HITLER'S WAR MACHINE

THE AFRIKA KORPS IN COMBAT

EDITED AND INTRODUCED BY
BOB CARRUTHERS

Pen & Sword
MILITARY

This edition published in 2013 by
Pen & Sword Military
An imprint of
Pen & Sword Books Ltd
47 Church Street
Barnsley
South Yorkshire
S70 2AS

First published in Great Britain in 2012 in digital format by
Coda Books Ltd.

Copyright © Coda Books Ltd, 2012
Published under licence by Pen & Sword Books Ltd.

ISBN 978 1 78159 134 5

A CIP catalogue record for this book is
available from the British Library

All rights reserved. No part of this book may be reproduced or transmitted in any form or by any means, electronic or mechanical including photocopying, recording or by any information storage and retrieval system, without permission from the Publisher in writing.

Printed and bound by
CPI Group (UK) Ltd, Croydon, CR0 4YY

Pen & Sword Books Ltd incorporates the Imprints of Pen & Sword Aviation, Pen & Sword Family History, Pen & Sword Maritime, Pen & Sword Military, Pen & Sword Discovery, Pen & Sword Politics, Pen & Sword Atlas, Pen & Sword Archaeology, Wharncliffe Local History, Wharncliffe True Crime, Wharncliffe Transport, Pen & Sword Select, Pen & Sword Military Classics, Leo Cooper, The Praetorian Press, Claymore Press, Remember When, Seaforth Publishing and Frontline Publishing

For a complete list of Pen & Sword titles please contact
PEN & SWORD BOOKS LIMITED
47 Church Street, Barnsley, South Yorkshire, S70 2AS, England
E-mail: enquiries@pen-and-sword.co.uk
Website: www.pen-and-sword.co.uk

CONTENTS

1. INTRODUCTION 6
2. THE AFRIKA KORPS 8
3. SUMMARY OF OPERATIONS IN NORTH AFRICA, 1940-1942 14
4. DEVELOPMENTS IN DESERT WARFARE 32
5. NOTES FROM THE NORTH AFRICAN THEATER 35
6. A TACTICAL STUDY OF THE EFFECTIVENESS OF THE GERMAN 88 MM ANTI-AIRCRAFT GUN AS AN ANTI-TANK WEAPON IN THE LIBYAN BATTLE 38
7. CONSTRUCTION OF A GERMAN BATTALION DEFENSE AREA IN NORTH AFRICA 43
8. OBSERVATIONS ON GERMAN ARTILLERY TACTICS 50
9. ARMORED FORCE TACTICS IN THE MIDDLE EAST 52
10. ENEMY ANTITANK MINE FIELDS AND BOOBY TRAPS IN AFRICA 58
11. EMPLOYMENT OF ANTIAIRCRAFT FORCES WITH A GERMAN PANZER DIVISION IN LIBYA 61
12. GERMAN SALVAGE PROCEDURE IN THE DESERT 64
13. OPERATIONS OF THE GERMAN TANK RECOVERY PLATOON 66
14. GERMAN TACTICS IN THE DESERT 69
15. INITIAL ACTION ON THE EL ALAMEIN LINE 72

16. GERMAN WIRE COMMUNICATION IN NORTH AFRICA 74
17. GERMAN ATTACK AT EL ALAMEIN 82
18. ENEMY MINEFIELDS AT EL ALAMEIN 95
19. AXIS MOTOR VEHICLES IN NORTH AFRICA 100
20. GERMAN PATROLS IN NORTH AFRICA 102
21. GERMAN AIR SUPPORT OF TANKS IN AFRICA 103
22. A GERMAN ANTITANK GUN EMPLACEMENT 105
23. GERMAN 88'S IN TUNISIA 107
24. ATTACK AGAINST GERMAN HEAVY TANK - PZKW 6 109
25. NOTES ON SECURITY FROM THE MIDDLE EAST .. 111
26. GERMAN MINE FIELDS IN LIBYA 116
27. SMALL-ARMS FIRE AGAINST LOW-FLYING AIRCRAFT 117
28. SECURITY MEASURES OF A GERMAN ARMORED DIVISION 118
29. GERMAN CONSTRUCTION AND DEVELOPMENT OF STRONGPOINT 120
30. SUMMARY AND EVALUATION OF OPERATIONS IN EGYPT 122
31. GERMAN 21ST ARMORED DIVISION - DIVISION SUPPLY 125
32. WATER SUPPLY OF A GERMAN TANK BATTALION IN LIBYA 126

MORE FROM THE SAME SERIES 128

Erwin Rommel in North Africa

1. INTRODUCTION

This book forms part of the series entitled 'Hitler's War Machine.' The aim is to provide the reader with a varied range of materials drawn from original writings covering the strategic, operational and tactical aspects of the weapons and battles of Hitler's war. The concept behind the series is to provide the well-read and knowledgeable reader with an interesting compilation of related primary sources combined with the best of what is in the public domain to build a picture of a particular aspect of that titanic struggle

I am pleased to report that the series has been well received and it is a pleasure to be able to bring original primary sources to the attention of an interested readership. I particularly enjoy discovering new primary sources, and I am pleased to be able to present them unadorned and unvarnished to a sophisticated audience. The primary sources such as Die Wehrmacht and Signal, speak for themselves and the readership I strive to serve is the increasingly well informed community of reader/historians which needs no editorial lead and can draw its own conclusions. I am well aware that our community is constantly striving to discover new nuggets of information, and I trust that with this volume I have managed to stimulate fresh enthusiasm and that at least some of these facts and articles will be new to you and will provoke readers to research further down these lines of investigation, and perhaps cause established views to be challenged once more. I am aware at all times in compiling these materials that our relentless pursuit of more and better historical information is at the core our common passion. I trust that this selection will contribute to that search and will help all of us to better comprehend and understand the bewildering events of the

Rommel arrives Tripoli during February 1941 and is greeted by Italian Officers.

last century.

In order to produce an interesting compilation giving a flavour of events at the tactical and operational level I have returned once more to the wartime US Intelligence series of pamphlets, which contain an intriguing series of contemporary articles on weapons and tactics. I find this series of pamphlets particularly fascinating as they are written in, what was then, the present tense and, as such, provide us with a sense of what was happening at the face of battle as events unfolded.

Thank you for buying this volume in the series we hope you will enjoy discovering some new insights you will go on to try the others in the series.

Bob Carruthers
Edinburgh 2012

2. THE AFRIKA KORPS

The German Africa Korps was known to the Germans, Die Deutsches Afrikakorps (DAK), or the Afrika Korps as it was popularly called, was the German expeditionary force which fought from 1941-43 in Libya and Tunisia during the North African Campaign of World War II. The reputation of the Afrika Korps is now synonymous with that of its first commander Erwin Rommel. As the size of the German deployment continued to expand Rommel later commanded the Panzer Army Africa which then evolved into the German-Italian Panzer Army (Deutsch-Italienische Panzerarmee) and finally to Army Group Africa. The Afrika Korps was a distinct and principal component throughout the North African campaign, and fought tenaciously against Allied forces until its surrender in May 1943.

ORGANIZATION

The Afrika Korps assembled for the first time in February 1941, and command devolved upon the shoulders of Erwin Rommel who was Adolf Hitler's personal choice to lead the formation. On 14th February Rommel himself landed on African soil in Libya to begin planning the campaign which would begin as soon his forces that could be brought into action.

The German Armed Forces High Command (Oberkommando der Wehrmacht, OKW) and Army High Command or (Oberkommando des Heeres, OKH) had decided to send a "blocking force" (Sperrverband) to Libya to support the Italian army. The Italian army group had been routed by Commonwealth Force's counter-offensive led by the British Eighth Army, in Operation Compass. The German "blocking force", commanded by Rommel, at first consisted of only the

5./leichte "Afrika" Panzer Regiment, which was quickly cobbled together from the second regiment of the 3./Panzer Division and various other small units attached for water treatment and medical care. These elements were organized into the 5th Light Division when they arrived in Africa from 10 February – 12 March 1941. In late April and into May, the 5th Light Division was joined by transference of the various elements constituting the 15th Panzer Division from Italy, though it did not completely arrive until after Rommel had made a counter-offensive and re-taken most of Cyrenaica and then subsequently gone back over to the defensive. At this time, the Afrikakorps consisted of the two divisions plus various smaller supporting units, and was officially subordinated to the Italian chain of command in Africa (though Rommel had conducted his offensive without any authorization).

On 15 August 1941, the German 5./leichte "Afrika" Division was redesignated 21st Panzer Division (commonly written as 21./PD), still attached to the enlarged entity still known as the Afrikakorps.

During the summer of 1941, the OKW and OKH invested more command structure in Africa by creating a new headquarters called Panzer Group Africa (Panzergruppe Afrika). On 15 August, Panzer Group Africa was activated with Rommel in command, and command of the Afrikakorps was turned over to Ludwig Crüwell. The Panzer Group controlled the Afrikakorps plus some additional German units that were sent to Africa, as well as two corps of Italian units. (A German "group" was approximately the equivalent of an army in other militaries, and in fact, Panzer Group Africa was redesignated as Panzer Army Africa (Panzerarmee Afrika) on 30 January 1942.)

After the defeat at El Alamein and the Allied invasion in Morocco and Algeria Operation Torch, the OKW once more upgraded its presence in Africa by creating the XC Army Corps in Tunisia on 19 November 1942, and then creating a new 5th

A DAK trooper with an anti-tank rifle, these weapons were fairly ineffective at anything but the shortest range.

Panzer Army headquarters there as well on 8 December, under the command of Colonel-General Hans-Jürgen von Arnim.

On 23 February 1943, Panzer Army Africa—now called the German-Italian Panzer Army—was redesignated as the Italian 1st Army and put under the command of Italian general Giovanni Messe, while Rommel was placed in command of a new Army Group Africa (Heeresgruppe Afrika), created to control both the Italian 1st Army and the 5th Panzer Army. The remnants of the Afrikakorps and other surviving units of the 1st Italian Army retreated into Tunisia. Command of the Army Group was turned over to von Arnim in March. On 13 May, remnants of the Afrikakorps surrendered, along with all other remaining Axis forces in North Africa.

COMPOSITION AND TERMINOLOGY

"Afrika Korps" is derived from the original German name properly written as one word. Strictly speaking, the term refers to the original formation which, although not dissolved, became part of the ever-expanding German and Italian presence in North Africa for its February 1941–May 1943 role in the North African Campaign. However, it is sometimes used by the news media and veteran Allied soldiers as a name for all the German units in North Africa. Some notable attached units include the 15th Panzer Division, 21st Panzer Division, Afrika zbV (zur besonderen Verwendung, "special purpose") Division, which was created as an infantry division and slowly upgraded to a fully motorized division, and then redesignated as the 90th Light Afrika Division; the 164th Light Afrika Division, the 999 Light "Afrika" Division, also the 334th Infantry division; and the Luftwaffenjäger-Brigade 1 or Fallschirmjäger-Ramcke Brigade Ramcke Parachute Brigade (named after its commander Hermann-Bernhard Ramcke). There were also eight Italian divisions (out of the 10 Italian Divisions in North Africa) under Rommel's command in Panzer Army Afrika, including two

An early 1941 image of the North Africa campaign - the crew are wearing the original tropical issue pith helmets.

armored divisions, two motorized divisions, three infantry divisions, and the Folgore parachute division. The army was supported by a number of smaller units from both the German and Italian armed forces.

The designation "Light" (German: Leicht) did not refer to a standardized table of organization and equipment (TOE) for the various German divisions that bore that designation.

German unit organizations were based on tables of organization, (Kriegsstärkenachweisungen, or KStN). Every unit in the German Army raised had one, and all orders raising units indicated the corresponding KStN number and date which applied to them. For instance, the 5./leichte "Afrika" or 5th Light "Africa" had an organizational structure that was missing specific elements to make it a complete Panzer "Division", as did its late April to May 1941 arriving "full complement" partner division in Africa, the 15./Panzer Division. The 5./le. "Africa" Division eventually became at least partially expanded into the 21./PD or 21st Panzer Division. It was given German unit elements that were already on the ground in North Africa and some replacement equipment to meet the prescribed full Panzer

Division KStN constraints (except for the Motorcycle Battalion component, which was never complete) and then renamed in August 1941. As the entire Afrikakorps organization was restructured and even renamed in August 1941, the nomenclature of Afrikakorps lasted less than six months. The famous force, with the short-lived name Afrikakorps, became a major German component of Panzer Army Africa; Panzerarmee Afrika, which evolved into the German-Italian Panzer Army (Deutsch-Italienische Panzerarmee) and then to Army Group Africa (Heeresgruppe Afrika) in the 27 months of the campaign for this force.

Additional German forces were sent to Africa and became components of the Panzer Army Africa, Panzerarmee Afrika. Examples such as the 164./le. "Africa" or 164th Light Afrika Division was at first only a partially-motorized infantry division, and actually never had any tanks at all, only armored cars and reconnaissance vehicles. Various German divisions in Africa occasionally reorganized or re-equipped without a change of name, or conversely were redesignated with a new name without any substantial reorganization. None of the German Armies actually fielded for service in North Africa completely met the service KStNs directed for their completion because of battle losses, sinkings across the Mediterranenan while in transit and the tremendous wear on the vehicles.

RAMCKE BRIGADE

The Luftwaffenjäger-Brigade 1, known more commonly as the Ramcke Parachute Brigade, worked alongside the Afrika Korps after Operation Hercules (the planned invasion of Malta) was cancelled and the Brigade was subsequently re-deployed to Germany.

3. SUMMARY OF OPERATIONS IN NORTH AFRICA, 1940-1942

The following U.S. military report on the battles in North Africa in 1940-1942 was originally published in Tactical and Technical Trends, No. 9, October 8th, 1942.

Marshal Graziani's offensive against Egypt in September 1940 was the first of five campaigns which have been fought over the Western Desert.

This first offensive, starting from Bardia on the Libyan-Egyptian border, pushed only as far as Sidi Barrani in Egypt before it was halted by the British. The first British offensive (second campaign), launched in December, crushed any hopes Graziani may have had of moving on to the Suez Canal, for Wavell's troops not only accomplished their objective of pushing the Italians over the border into Libya, but moved on across Cyrenaica as far as El Agheila, where over-extended lines of

A DAK command half track is parked among vehicles of the Panzer division May 1941.

communication finally halted the drive in February 1941. The second Axis drive (third campaign), against British forces depleted by withdrawals from the Balkan Campaign, introduced Rommel's Afrika Korps, which, with the Italians, drove the British to the frontier during March and April of 1941. Apart from the Battle of Salum in June, the front was relatively quiet, until the second British offensive (fourth campaign) in November 1941 again carried them to El Agheila, only to be pushed back by a heavy counterattack (January 1942) to the Gazala-Bir Hacheim line. In May of this year, Rommel attacked (fifth campaign) and forced a British retreat to the present Alamein positions.

In all this fighting, no clear-cut decision has been reached. Despite Axis domination of most of the Mediterranean, Britain still holds the Middle East, since a reinforced Eighth Army, massed on the short Alamein line, blocks Rommel's path to the Nile Delta.

The desert has not only been the scene of a struggle for strategic control of the Mediterranean and the Middle East; it has also been a closely watched proving ground for tactics, techniques, and equipment—"a tactician's paradise and a quartermaster's hell." These subjects have been discussed in detail in this and other Military Intelligence Service publications; the following resume of the fighting is intended only to summarize the five campaigns as a background for the future operations in this theater.

THE FIRST CAMPAIGN

The long-expected Italian assault on Egypt began on September 14, 1940. The advancing forces consisted of two mechanized columns of light and medium tanks heavily supported by artillery. The campaign, however, was of the nature of a British withdrawal rather than an Italian advance, and Salum, Buq Buq and Sidi Barrani were occupied by the Italians in a few days and without heavy fighting. Apparently the need for additional preparations prevented Graziani from attempting to push on to the next logical objective, the British railhead at Mersa Matruh.

THE SECOND CAMPAIGN

Forced to stop at Sidi Barrani, Graziani disposed his troops as follows: the 1st Libyan and 101st Blackshirt Divisions occupied Sidi Barrani itself and positions about 15 miles east of it. The 2d Libyan Division occupied positions extending some 16 miles south of Sidi Barrani, while the 63d Metropolitan Division covered the escarpment from a point north of Rabia westward for about 18 miles. The 62d Metropolitan Division occupied Fort Capuzzo and, with the 104th Blackshirt Division, Salum.

Either the Italians assumed their defensive positions to be only temporary, or else they showed a rather naive concept of fortifications and security measures. All camp perimeters were clearly marked by loose stonewalls about 2 feet high with a 2-foot trench in front. Little barbed wire was used, and along the perimeters, in line, were strung the rifles, mortars, machine guns, antitank guns, artillery, and grenades. Defense in depth, mutually supporting fire, outposts, and patrols were all lacking. Troops, stores, and equipment were kept inside the perimeter.

British troops, consisting of the 7th Armored Division (including two tank brigades and a support group) and the 4th Indian Division (3d and 11th Indian Brigades and 16th British Brigade), prepared to attack. The objective was to isolate and destroy all Italian troops east of a gap between the escarpment and the southern positions of the 2d Libyan Division. On December 9, 48 infantry tanks, followed by the 3d Indian Infantry Brigade on trucks, moved in against the northwestern perimeter of the southern positions at 0800. Although the British tanks met heavy defensive fire, they broke through the perimeter into the middle of a group of 25 Italian tanks, which they managed to neutralize. Indian infantry moved in after the tanks,

A column of Panzer III tanks on the move towards the front during May 1941.

proceeded to mop up, and captured about 4,000 officers and men. By afternoon, infantry tanks and the 11th Indian Infantry Brigade had moved north and captured 7,000 more prisoners in other positions south of Sidi Barrani.

The next British move was a direct assault on Sidi Barrani itself, executed by the three brigades of the 4th Indian Division from the south and southwest, and the 4th Armored Brigade from the west. A simultaneous move on Maktila was made unnecessary by the withdrawal of its garrison into the Sidi Barrani fortifications.

The attack was highly successful; the British captured 15,000 officers and men, while the 7th Armored Brigade and Support Group moved to the vicinity of Buq Buq, where operations against retiring Italian columns took 12,000 to 14,000 more prisoners.

Italian columns were attacked during the 12th by British tanks and armored cars, while the infantry of the 4th Indian Division spent most of its time attempting to handle the flood of prisoners.

Positions around Rabia were being abandoned, and the retreating Italians poured into the frontier defenses of Halfaya,

Capuzzo, and Salum. RAF fighters attacked the retiring enemy while bombers dropped heavy loads on Bardia and Tobruk. At the frontier, the enemy defenses stiffened, and the Italian Air Force began effective action against the advancing British. Salum was taken on the 13th, however, and on the 14th, British armored-car patrols of the 7th Armored Division and the Free French bypassed Bardia to cut the coastal road to Tobruk.

Bardia was still intact, except for damages from heavy bombing, and on the 16th the Italian frontier forces withdrew into its defenses, after evacuating their remaining positions in the Salum-Capuzzo-Halfaya area. From the 17th to the 21st; the 7th Armored Division and the Support Group moved to reinforce the patrol on the Tobruk road and to prevent a retreat from Bardia.

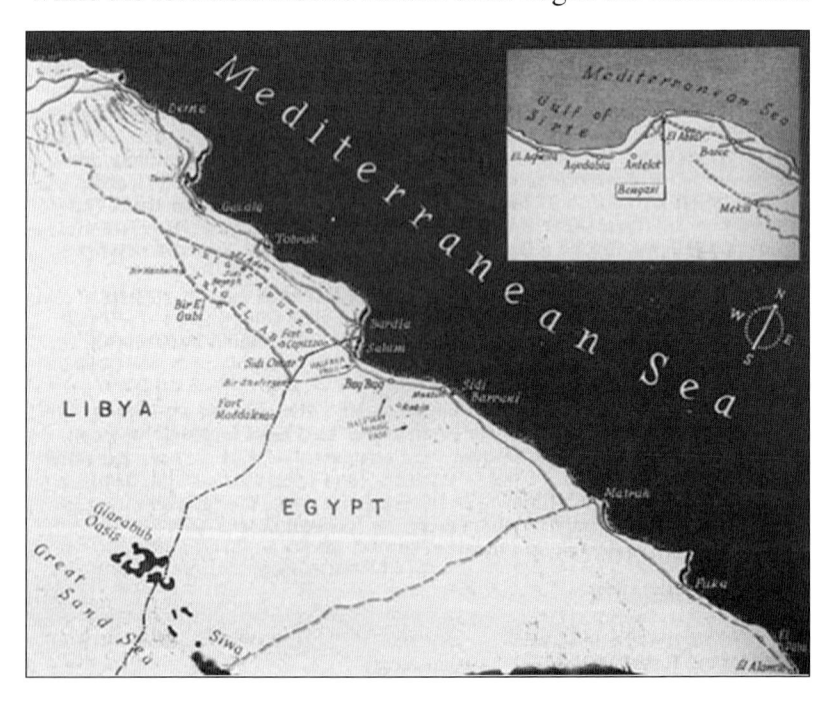

Bardia itself was fortified by three belts, consisting of a number of mines, concrete bunkers, and tank traps in addition to the familiar loose stone walls of the Sidi Barrani fortifications. While the foremost mobile British units began the encirclement of Tobruk, and the RAF bombed Bir el Gubi, Gazala, Tmimi, Derna, and Tripoli, the British prepared to assault Bardia. Elements of the 7th Armored Division blocked the road from Bardia to Tobruk, and the 16th British Brigade, plus the newly arrived Australians, attacked the southern perimeter at dawn on January 3, while the Support Group of the 7th Armored Division contained the western defenses. Because of the stronger antitank defense, infantry and engineers preceded the tanks in the attack. Different sectors surrendered individually, but it was not until January 5 that the last Italians in the coastal area stopped fighting. Total prisoners for the operation amounted to 32,000 men.

British forces were already being reduced by withdrawals to Greece, but the British decided to push on. The Bardia attack had proved successful, and the same tactics, preceded by the reduction of outposts outside the actual perimeter, brought the fall of Tobruk. The British captured 20,000 Italians at the capitulation of that city on January 21.

The campaign's high spot came, however, on February 4, when the 7th Armored Division made a 150-mile dash from Mekili to Antelat, completely surprised the Italians retreating from Bengasi, and decisively defeated them. The campaign ended with the occupation of El Agheila a few days later.

THE THIRD CAMPAIGN

The advance elements of the German Afrika Korps debarked at Tripoli on February 12, and it soon became obvious that an offensive would be undertaken against the weakened British forces.

By March 31, when the Axis offensive actually started, British forces in Cyrenaica consisted only of about 40 armored cars, one armored brigade of 75 tanks (of which two-thirds were obsolescent light tanks or captured Italian tanks), 5 battalions of infantry, 3 weak regiments of light artillery, and a few antitank and antiaircraft guns—hardly a force to meet the threatened Axis offensive. When the Germans struck with a frontal attack on the forward British infantry positions in the north, and an enveloping attack along the edge of the salt marshes in the south, the British were forced to withdraw through Antelat to a position about 30 miles east of Bengasi. In addition to fighting rear-guard actions, the British had to contend with the difficulty of providing transportation from an extremely limited supply of trucks.

Communications had also broken down, and the armored brigade, as well as the 3d Motorized Indian Brigade in the vicinity of Mekili, was out of contact most of the time with headquarters. By April 6, German armored columns were advancing on the British left flank, where they engaged the Indian Brigade and threatened to outflank the main British force. The armored brigade had not arrived to reinforce the Indian brigade as planned, having followed the main body of British troops on to the coastal road; the Indian Brigade was defeated, and with the left flank gone, withdrawal all the way to the frontier was undertaken.

The withdrawal continued until the Axis forces had taken Salum and Halfaya Pass, leaving only an isolated Tobruk in the hands of the British.

THE BATTLE OF SALUM

The Axis attitude of passive defense, and reports of substantial withdrawals of German air strength from the Middle East, led the British into a decision to attack on June 15, 1941, in an attempt to destroy the German and Italian forces in the frontier area and relieve the besieged garrison of Tobruk. The British units available for this attack were considerably weaker than the total German and Italian forces in the Tobruk and frontier sectors, particularly in tanks and antitank guns. However, it was hoped that the Axis frontier defenses would be destroyed before reinforcements from the Tobruk area could be brought up. The British attackers were divided into three main groups: a Coastal

An Me 109 is prepared for take-off in North Arica during 1941.

Force, consisting of a brigade of Indian infantry, one platoon of tanks, an antitank company, and one regiment of light and medium artillery; an Escarpment Force, composed of an armored brigade, a battalion and a half of infantry, a regiment of field artillery, and antiaircraft and antitank units; and, third, an armored brigade group supported by a brigade of infantry. The first of these forces was to attack the Halfaya Pass position from along the coast, below the escarpment. This attack was to be supported by a portion of the Escarpment Force (second column) from above. The third column, with the remainder of the Escarpment Force was to move on toward the fortified positions along the border and then attack Fort Capuzzo and Salum.

Except for the failure of the Coastal Force to capture the Halfaya Pass position, the British plans for the initial phases were carried out successfully. The Escarpment Force, made up of the 4th Indian Division and a tank brigade, with other units attached, proceeded to the wire fence at the Libyan-Egyptian border and launched successful attacks on small fortified areas and on Fort Capuzzo and Salum. The 7th Armored Brigade and the Support Group protected the left flank of the 4th Indian

The crew of this Luftwaffe BMW motorcycle and side car combination grab some much needed rest during the advance of April 1941.

Division as ordered. The 7th Armored Brigade, however, was driven out of its position in the northwestern sector by superior numbers of tanks of the 15th German Armored Division, and the Support Group in the southwestern sector was outnumbered by the motorized and armored forces of the 5th German Light Motorized Division, which included a battalion of 86 tanks.

Threatened with an enveloping movement against his weakening flank, the commander of the 4th Indian Division was forced to withdraw in order to prevent his lines of supply and communication from being cut. The decision to withdraw was also influenced by the fact that the Coastal Force on the right flank, in spite of determined assaults, had been unable to take the Halfaya Pass position and join the forward units. The withdrawal was completed on the night of June 17. The Axis forces did not pursue the retreating British, probably because the opening of the German offensive against Russia was only 5 days off.

THE FOURTH CAMPAIGN

By the middle of November, the British Eighth Army had accumulated the requisite strength for an offensive, and on the night of November 17-18 the British 7th Armored Division, the 1st New Zealand Infantry Division, and the 1st South African Division (less one brigade) crossed the frontier wire to attempt an enveloping movement against the German armored troops lying between the Axis-held Salum area and the British fortress of Tobruk. The 4th Indian Division was given the mission of containing the Axis forces in the heavily defended frontier triangle, which included Bardia, Sidi Omar, Salum, and Halfaya Pass. From the 19th to the 23d, Axis and British tanks (including one brigade of 166 light U.S. M3's) battled to gain armored superiority, while the Tobruk garrison began, on November 21, to fight its way out of the ring of Italian infantry in an attempt to make contact with the British armored and infantry forces in the Sidi Rezegh area.

On the first day of fighting, November 19, the British 22d Armored Brigade successfully engaged the Italian Ariete Armored Division at Bir el Gubi. Meanwhile, the 7th Armored Brigade and 7th Support Group moved toward Sidi Rezegh, and the 4th Armored Brigade, with American tanks, engaged strong German tank units halfway between Bir el Gubi and the Omars. This dispersion of British armored forces was, perhaps, the most serious mistake of the campaign, for it enabled Rommel to strike the British units in detail and thus neutralized the initial British numerical superiority. By the night of November 21, the British tank units had been brought together at Sidi Rezegh, but by that time they were so depleted that the concentration brought little striking power.

During the tank actions, the 1st New Zealand Division had moved north and northeast, around the Omars, into Fort Capuzzo on November 20, and on to the Tobruk-Bardia road the next day. One brigade was left behind to contain Bardia, and the remainder of the division started to fight its way along the coastal road toward Tobruk, where they were to assist the garrison's attempt to break out.

The 4th Indian Division, in the frontier area, attacked and reduced the fortified Omars position on November 22. One infantry brigade, two squadrons of heavy infantry tanks, and most of the division artillery, used in the action were which netted much Axis materiel and equipment, and about 3,600 prisoners.

At the end of the armored battles, the Axis armored units were also heavily depleted; two days were spent in harrassing activities, until, late on the 24th, Rommel gathered all his remaining tank strength and made a drive toward the Omar-Sheferzen area. This seriously disrupted the British rear-area installations and caused a great deal of confusion, although few casualties resulted. Inconclusive actions continued throughout the next few days while the British brought in tank reinforcements and made repairs.

Finally, on November 26, the New Zealanders made contact with the Tobruk garrison, causing Rommel to withdraw his tanks to the north in an attempt to separate the Sidi Rezegh and Tobruk forces, which he did on December 1 and 2. More British reinforcements arrived, however, and, as the Indians and South Africans mopped up isolated resistances in the battle area, the strengthened 7th Armored Division renewed activities against enemy tank and infantry units.

It became obvious by December 6 that Rommel was withdrawing to the west, where he attempted to establish fortified positions: first, between El Adem and Bir el Gubi; and a few days later, in the Gazala area. These were finally reduced by December 16, and the Axis troops continued to withdraw, fighting successive rearguard actions until finally on January 7 the British occupied Agedabia.

On January 2, the 2d South African Division had made a highly successful tank and infantry attack on the isolated Axis troops in Bardia, taking 8,500 prisoners and liberating 1,150 British troops. A short time later Salum, and then Halfaya Pass,

The heavy artillery awaits the call to action, Libya April 1941.

fell to the South African infantry after the isolated and weakened garrisons had been subjected to extensive and heavy bombardment by artillery and air.

The British 22d Armored Brigade had suffered heavily at Agedabia on December 28, and when the 2d Armored Brigade was defeated near Antelat on January 23, the position of the Eighth Army in the Bengasi area became untenable, and General Ritchie decided to withdraw to the east. There the British set up a mined and fortified line extending from Gazala to Bir Hacheim and started to build up strength for a new offensive. Axis troops also prepared for renewed attack, and little activity took place until the fifth campaign started on the night of May 26.

THE FIFTH CAMPAIGN

With his mobile Afrika Korps, Rommel moved around the fortified position of Bir Hacheim to attack the British armored units in rear of their minefield. Both of the German armored divisions and the 90th Light Division were used in the complete envelopment. The Italian Ariete Armored Division and Trieste Motorized Division halted at the southern end of the minefield to attack Bir Hacheim on the morning of May 27. The British,

Rommel and Bayerlein survey the harbour of Tobruk shortly after its capture in June 1942.

who had been led by extensive Axis demonstrations to expect a frontal assault in the northern sector, were not entirely prepared for the flanking attack; the 4th Armored Brigade, one motorized infantry brigade, Headquarters of the 7th Armored Division, and some elements of the 22d Armored Brigade were struck in detail by the German columns before they could be concentrated to repulse the attack.

The 1st Free French Brigade at Bir Hacheim successfully repulsed the initial Italian attack, destroying some 30 to 50 enemy tanks.

During the next few days, heavy fighting continued east of the British positions, and slowly the British pushed most of the German armored forces against the rear of the minefields. By May 29 the supply situation of the Axis armored forces was growing acute, for the RAF, the 7th Support Group, and Free French at Bir Hacheim were effectively neutralizing all attempts to move supplies around the southern flank. Although the Italian Trieste Division had managed to open two small gaps opposite the armored concentrations in the Knightsbridge area, the British were moving to close this gap and did not feel that such narrow corridors could be effectively used for supply.

The Germans, realizing the necessity for opening an adequate route through the minefields, circled their armored forces in the so-called Cauldron with a number of antitank guns, and, turning their back to the British armored forces, they effectively attacked and destroyed British infantry units attempt to close the gaps. It would seem logical for the British to have struck the Axis armored forces from the rear with all available strength while this action was going on, but the British attack was delayed, and the initial gaps were widened the point where they could be used for supply.

Indecisive fighting now took place for the next few days while the Germans first withdrew to the west through the gap, and then returned.

The next major action was the assault on Bir Hacheim. During the first week in June this position had been subjected to increasingly severe attacks by the Italians and some units of the German Armored Forces. Stuka dive bombers, heavy artillery (up to 210-mm), and concentrations of tanks were now used in an effort to reduce the fortifications. Realizing that this former flank position was no longer of any value to the British, General Ritchie gave orders on June 10 that it be abandoned. Heavy casualties resulted during the difficult evacuation, and by the time the Free French rejoined the British units only one-half remained of the original garrison of 5,000.

With the fall of the Free French position, the Germans units immediately fanned out in rear of the British, who were now forced to withdraw. The 1st South African and 50th British Divisions in the north were to be withdrawn along the coastal road to Tobruk, and all available British armored units were detailed to protect the southern flank for this withdrawal. This defensive line stretched from the Knightsbridge "box"; held by the 200th Guards Brigade, to El Adem.

By this disposition, British armored units were tied down along an extended line and deprived of their mobility. This gave Rommel his chance to achieve a much-needed numerical superiority in tanks.

The British tanks attacked at dawn June 12, moving south from the escarpment. The groups of German tanks, however, successfully drew the British armor onto the 88-mm and 50-mm guns which were hidden in practically every small wadi, and among groups of derelict vehicles. After losing a number of cruiser tanks and American mediums, the British withdrew to their previous line along the escarpment. The Germans, attempting to conserve their own tanks, did not attack, but successfully brought their antitank guns within range of the British by sending forward one or two tanks which would weave back and forth and create a cloud of dust behind which the

A Panzer III with the 37mm main armament rolls past a blazing British tank, North Africa, 1941.

antitank guns were brought up. After the dust settled, the antitank guns would open fire at ranges of 1,000 to 1,400 yards. In firing at the American mediums, Axis guns concentrated on the vulnerable tracks and suspension system.

In addition to these new tactics, the Germans continued to lure British tanks onto emplaced antitank guns by sending forth small motorized infantry units as bait.

During the night the British tanks withdrew from the escarpment across the Trig Capuzzo, and took up positions before Acroma which they were to defend from direct Axis attack as long as possible.

On June 13 the battle continued, while the Guards Brigade evacuated the Knightsbridge box and took up positions near Acroma. The tank battle continued throughout the day with the Axis utilizing antitank guns rather than their armor; by the end of the day the British had lost all but 65 of the 300 or more tanks with which they had started on the day before.

In addition to these intensive ground operations, Axis dive-bombers attacked the British battle positions almost continuously during June 12.

The British were now forced to withdraw at least to the Libyan-Egyptian frontier, but after some debate it was decided that an attempt should be made to hold Tobruk. The situation, however, was not exactly comparable to that of the previous year when Rommel first pushed south of that fortress and isolated it. Because of a greater Axis control of the Mediterranean, the Royal Navy could no longer undertake to supply the port, and the German and Italian land forces were strong enough this time to make a determined assault on the fortress. In Tobruk were left the 2d South African Division, the Guards Brigade, the 11th Indian Brigade, one Brigade of the 1st South African Division, and at least five regiments of artillery. The main body of the British Eighth Army withdrew to the frontier.

Advance elements of the 90th Light Division pushed on toward Bardia and Sidi Omar; the main German and Italian forces prepared to assault Tobruk. The attack was preceded by intense dive-bombing and artillery preparation, and on June 20 Axis troops penetrated the southern sector; a few hours later a larger force pushed into the city itself through the Derna-road gap in the minefields. The surrender has been reported to have come some time in the middle of the morning, but many British units continued to resist, and the attacking forces did not reach the harbor area until the middle of the afternoon.

With Tobruk gone, the main Axis forces pushed on toward the British frontier positions, and after brief fighting in that area the British decided to withdraw to Mersa Matruh where, reinforced by the New Zealand Division, they hoped to be able to make a stand.

On June 26 Rommel's two armored divisions and the 90th Light Division pushed in the British covering forces and prepared to encircle and attack Matruh. Again the British decided that the impending encirclement presented too much danger, and, now under the direct command of General Auchinleck, what was left of the Elghh Army withdrew to the present position on the El Alamein line. Some British units were captured in the Matruh evacuation. By June 30, both sides had reached a line extending from El Alamein to the Qattara Depression. Heavy fighting raged along this line for several days, but because of stiffened British resistance and the Axis drive's loss of momentum, Rommel failed to advance further.

Since that time intermittent fighting to gain control of the "hills" of the position has taken place but neither side has attempted an all-out offensive.

4. DEVELOPMENTS IN DESERT WARFARE

1. TANK AND ARTILLERY TACTICS

The Germans have developed a new method of combining tanks with 88-mm and 50-mm guns for an attack. The procedure is for a wave of tanks to charge in close to a United Nations position and then crisscross until a dense cloud of dust rises. After this, a second wave of tanks comes up in the dust, accompanied by the 88-mms and the 50-mms, which entrench themselves in wadis or, wherever possible, behind abandoned vehicles. While the dust is settling, the guns open fire from these close ranges with considerable effect. The Germans rarely ever fire directly at the front of opposing tanks; they wait for angle shots and try to hit the tanks on the side.

2. BREAKING TRAILS THROUGH MINEFIELDS

The Germans have two methods for going through minefields:

(a) They lay a smoke screen and send in engineers to plot a trail through the minefield, locate mines in the passageway with mine detectors, and detonate the charges.

(b) Or, behind an artillery barrage, they send a tank over the trail selected. The tank goes ahead until its tracks are blown off by exploding mines. A second tank then tows the first one out, and resumes the forward drive until its own tracks, in turn, are damaged. A third then comes to tow the second, and the process is repeated until a trail through the minefield has been established. The Germans usually get through at a cost of three or four tanks. Since the only damage these suffer is the loss of their tracks—which the German recovery system can repair in three or four hours—the Germans do not regard minefields as serious obstacles in the desert. It should be noted that the Germans use anything and everything to pull

The difficulty of supplying the Afrika Korps can be seen from this 1941 study of the trucks trundling their way to the front.

tanks off the field. The recovery and maintenance system operating in Libya has been so well developed that it can repair 10 tanks a day.

3. AIR-GROUND RECOGNITION

The Germans usually have accurate air-ground recognition. First, ground troops release a chemical smoke, often pink, which can be seen at 10,000 feet. Artillery then fires on the target. Planes observe the fire and bomb the area where the shells are falling.

4. SLIT TRENCHES

It has been found that slit trenches are an absolute necessity in case of bombing or artillery fire. Personnel in them are in very little danger from bombers unless they score a direct hit on the trench.

5. TRANSPORTATION

There are few long marches in the desert; nearly everything is now on wheels. On or near the front there are some foot movements, but even these are not practical over long periods. Thousands of trucks must be used, creating special problems.

Vehicles behind the lines are not dug in, but scattered at least 200 yards apart. Thus arranged, they make poor targets for aircraft since it is impossible to damage two trucks with a single bomb—and bombs are too expensive to use one per vehicle.

Excepting a small section for the driver to see through, the windshields of trucks are often greased lightly so that the dust will blow against them and stick. Sometimes they are painted. This prevents the windshield from reflecting light. The windshields are necessary to protect personnel from wind and dust.

In the daytime most trucks are kept out of artillery range.

6. SUPPLY

The Germans advance with supplies for 5 days in their trucks. On the fifth day the emptied trucks turn back, and a freshly loaded group replaces them.

7. EFFECT OF WEATHER

Most German soldiers are accustomed to temperate weather, and have to adapt themselves to the dry desert heat. To United States soldiers from Texas, Arizona, New Mexico, and the California valleys, dry heat is no novelty. Military observers agree that the heat of the African desert, although not the last word in comfort, has been exaggerated by newspaper correspondents.

5. NOTES FROM THE NORTH AFRICAN THEATER

Miscellaneous notes on German tactics and weapons in North Africa, from the Intelligence Bulletin, December 1942.

1. ARMORED-CAR TACTICS
Questioning of German reconnaissance-unit prisoners reveals the following information about armored-car tactics:
- Antitank guns moving on self-propelled mounts have advanced at times with the armored cars.
- When attacked by low-flying aircraft, only the 4-wheeled vehicles engage with fire from their open turrets; 8-wheel cars, lacking open turrets, cannot fire.
- The commander of an armored-car reconnaissance patrol always moves in the leading armored car.

2. AMMUNITION SUPPLY FOR TANKS
It is reported that trucks no longer go well forward to supply tanks with ammunition. Trucks now unload out of range of enemy artillery and establish small dumps, which can be cleared in a day. Drivers unload their own vehicles, no extra personnel being allotted for this purpose. Wherever possible, these dumps are located under cover of rising ground, and the tanks come back to the dumps for fresh supplies of ammunition.

3. TANK TACTICS
German tank tactics are very flexible. Often a local commander can vary them, according to his own ideas and local circumstances. No tank opens fire until it is definitely sure of the identity of the target. German tanks advance on the enemy at full speed until they are within 200 to 300 yards; at this point they halt temporarily and fire. The operation demands a high degree of self-control, but the compensating factor is that a much

A knocked out Panzer III with track damage near El Alamein 1942.

larger percentage of hits can be scored from a stationary tank than from a moving tank.

4. TANK REPAIRS

Each tank battalion carries seven fully qualified tank mechanics. The regiment has a small repair shop, with adequate spares, which follows very closely behind the fighting units. Eighty percent of all tank repairs are made on the battlefield, but if a tank has to go back to its base, it is usually taken on a recovery vehicle.

5. ARMAMENT

The total number of shells carried by a Mark III tank is 80. Previous information indicated that 100 rounds were carried.

6. RADIO COMMUNICATION

Intercommunication between units ranging in size from the battalion to the regiment is on medium wave lengths. Intercommunication between units lower than the battalion is on short wave lengths. All wave lengths are allotted by the division, and are changed frequently.

7. LATEST INTERROGATION PROCEDURE

No formal questioning of prisoners regarding tactics is carried out by leading combat elements. As soon as prisoners have been captured, they are searched and then dispatched to division headquarters for tactical interrogation by division intelligence officers. The officer or noncom in charge of the front-line troops who have taken the prisoners goes alone to the rear, ahead of the captured men. He takes with him all captured documents, and informs division intelligence officers as to the local tactical situation so that they will be well equipped to examine the prisoners. If possible, he also attends the interrogation.

6. A TACTICAL STUDY OF THE EFFECTIVENESS OF THE GERMAN 88 MM ANTI-AIRCRAFT GUN AS AN ANTI-TANK WEAPON IN THE LIBYAN BATTLE

Recent cables from American military observers in Cairo and at the front with the Eighth British Army in Libya stress the important role being played by the German 88 MM anti-aircraft gun in the ground phase of the desert battles now in progress.

The effectiveness of this weapon as a tank destroyer was rather clearly apparent in the course of the November and December British Libyan offensive. One of our observers at that time stated in an official report that the 88 MM was the most feared weapon which the British tanks had to face, and that the destruction wrought by it, on both chassis and turret of the British tanks, was incomparably greater than that caused by any other Axis weapon.

The characteristics of this gun are as follows:
- Muzzle velocity: 2750 feet per second
- Weight of shell: 19.8 pounds
- Vertical range: 37,000 feet
- Horizontal range: 16,000 yards
- Weight in firing position: 5.2 tons
- The gun is tractor drawn.
- It is provided with a steel shield of unknown thickness.

An American military observer who had many opportunities to witness this gun in Germany in 1940, speaks of this weapon as follows:

"The 88 MM is basically a gun for firing on moving targets.

A fine study of the fearsome 88mm dual purpose ant-aircraft and anti-tank gun in road transit mode.

The crew is also specially trained for firing on highly rapid moving targets, primarily on airplanes. The whole control apparatus is designed for fast moving targets with a very rapid rate of fire: 25 rounds per minute. The gun is capable of great volume fire and extreme accuracy against moving targets of any type. It is equally efficient on targets on the ground as well as in the air. For attacks on armored vehicles, it is provided with a special armor-piercing shell."

The German 88 MM anti-aircraft gun was designed and constructed in secret in the ten year period prior to the advent of Hitler, when the German army was subject to rigid personnel and material limitations. It is known that it was the plan of its designers to construct a dual purpose anti-aircraft and anti-tank weapon. The anti-tank purpose of the weapon was, however, veiled in secrecy and the German intentions in this regard did not become known to the world until the Polish campaign of 1939.

However, so definitely was the Axis attitude offensive, not only in Poland but in the French campaign of 1940, as well, that United Nations observers did not grasp at the time the full

Aiming the heavy artillery on the Tunisian front 1943.

significance and effectiveness of this weapon.

Commencing in 1940, the Germans began to provide these guns with an armored shield in order to protect its personnel against small arms bullets as well as smaller anti-tank projectiles.

It appears that this weapon has played an important role throughout the Russian campaign. However, far more exact information is available as to its use in Libya, than on the Russian battlefields.

In November 1941, when Gen. Auchinleck launched his major offensive, Marshal Rommel, his opponent, created three tank proof localities along his front line: at Bardia, Sollum and in the vicinity of Halfia pass. The defenses of each of these strong points were built around a battalion (12) of 88 MM AA guns, so sighted as to provide all around protection. These guns were supported by a large number of smaller anti-tank weapons. So well organized were these strong points that they were never seriously attacked, and only fell when the British had pushed on to Benghazi and when the water and food stocks of the strong points became exhausted. The British ascribe the long resistance put up by these strong points to the difficulty they found in coping with these dual purpose weapons.

In the battle now raging in Libya, Rommel's offensive use of these weapons is of considerable interest. The anti-aircraft guns appear to follow closely his armored vehicles. As soon as the front begins to stabilize, the 88 MM AA guns go into position and around them is then organized a "tank proof" locality. The German tanks are then withdrawn for offensive operations elsewhere.

The effectiveness of these weapons is clearly brought out from the following quotations from reports of observers now at the front in the desert battle around Tobruk:

One report includes the following statement:

"The German 88 MM guns penetrate the armour of all British tanks. British tanks dare not attack them. Up to now the British seem incapable of dealing with these weapons."

Another observer reports as follows:

"At a point in the Knightsbridge area, the 4th British armored brigade faced some 35 German tanks of the Mark III and IV type drawn up in line and obviously inviting attack. These tanks were supported by a battalion of anti-aircraft guns. The commander of the 4th Brigade refused to attack at all because of the presence of these guns on the battlefield.

"Slight firing occurred throughout the day. Towards evening the superior British tank force withdrew and the German tanks attacked after nightfall in a new direction. Their 88 MM guns had checked the British all day and permitted Rommel to seize the initiative as soon as the British threat had vanished."

Still a third report reads as follows:

"The greatest single tank destroyer is the German 88 MM anti-aircraft gun. For example, on May 27th at 8:00 A.M., Axis forces having enveloped Bir Hacheim, a German tank force of sixty tanks attacked the British 22nd Brigade some distance to the northeast. The British moved to attack this force with 50 light and medium American tanks. It soon became apparent that this British force was inadequate and the Brigadier commanding ordered a second regiment of 50 tanks into action. In ten minutes the 88 MM German AA guns destroyed 8 American medium tanks of this reinforcing regiment. All day thereafter, the British engaged the enemy half-heartedly and finally withdrew. Sixteen American medium tanks were lost in all. These sixteen fell victims without a single exception to the 88 MM AA gun."

7. CONSTRUCTION OF A GERMAN BATTALION DEFENSE AREA IN NORTH AFRICA

A report on WWII German defense areas in North Africa, from Tactical and Technical Trends, No. 31, August 12th, 1943.

As stated in Tactical and Technical Trends, No. 27, p. 21, the German doctrine as applied to defense calls for the concentration of the available forces in a few, very strong islands of resistance. In contrast to the pre-1940 French "linear" practice of setting up the defense in platoon "strong-points" supported by field artillery in the rear, Major F. O. Miksche a well known Czech military writer, pointed out in "Blitzkrieg" published in 1942 that the Germans favor the use of defense areas containing at least a rifle company, reinforced by appropriate supporting weapons, organized for all-around defense, wired-in behind mine fields, and provided with their own infantry artillery. Even

A pair of Panzer II light tanks preparing to move forward. Libya 1942.

a battalion may be employed in one of these positions, which, when developed to their fullest extent, are self-sustaining defense areas, capable of resisting armored attack. An example of such an island of resistance will be found in the following translation of a German document entitled "Training Publication for the Installation of Battalion Defense Areas" issued by the Commander-in-Chief of the Panzer Army in Africa. A combat officer very recently returned from southern Tunisia reports that defenses of this type were met with there.

***

In order to strengthen the power of defense, the troops will organize defense areas which they can hold against attacks coming from any direction.

A. DIMENSIONS

The normal battalion front in a defensive position may be from 3,500 to 4,000 yards; company defense areas (see figure 1) are some 700 yards wide by 300 in depth, and spaced about 500 yards apart.

B. GARRISON OF COMPANY POSITIONS

A battalion sector is divided into several company defense areas. In general, a rifle company with infantry heavy weapons attached occupies each of the four sub-defense areas. The unit command posts are also to be installed within these defense areas. Artillery is stationed behind the forward company defense areas on terrain protected by the rear company defense area of the battalion sector.

[Note: Whether this artillery is composed of the infantry guns, or attached field artillery is not clear but field artillery was found in such defense areas in Tunisia. Obviously, while the lay-out is such that infantry guns could cover the forward company positions, some field guns of greater range could be used, if available.]

C. WEAPONS

Weapons are distributed so as to give mutual supporting fire.

Every company defense area is provided with infantry light and heavy weapons. Armor-piercing weapons, and antiaircraft guns are attached.

D. DEFENSES

The company defense area is to be fenced in with wire. However, platoon areas within such company areas are not to be inclosed by wire. *[Note: Perhaps sufficient wire for both inside and outside entanglements was not available as wired-in platoon areas have been encountered.]* The distance of the wire entanglements from the most forward weapons is about 50 to 100 yards.

To facilitate reconnaissance activity, narrow lanes through the wire entanglements are to be laid out on the enemy side. Wide lanes are permitted only on the flanks.

To defend the protective minefields, and wire entanglements, rifle pits, listening posts, observation posts, and weapon emplacements are installed. Dug-outs are constructed for the garrison of the area.

Communication trenches are to be dug only between the firing positions or observation posts and nearby dugouts. Extensive communication trenches give the attacking enemy a chance to gain a foothold inside. In stony terrain the parapet is to be made of sandbags or stone, but trenches must first be dug deep enough into the ground (by blasting, if necessary) to prevent the position from showing above the surface.

As a matter of principle, no installations, as seen from the enemy side, must stand out above the surface of the grounds. Defended areas are not to be laid out on the crests of ridges but on the slopes [whether forward or reverse slopes, is not made clear]. Although the highest positions are normally the most desirable for observation and antiaircraft purposes, such installations must not be placed on forward slopes in view of the enemy, but somewhat further to the rear, masked by the crest.

Dummy positions (also for artillery and antiaircraft) are to be used for the purpose of diverting enemy artillery fire. Distance from the other positions must be great enough to protect the latter from the natural dispersion of artillery fire.

The sections of trenches inside a position must have frequent traverses or angles to reduce the splintering effect (see figure 2). Good camouflage is the best protection against enemy fire.

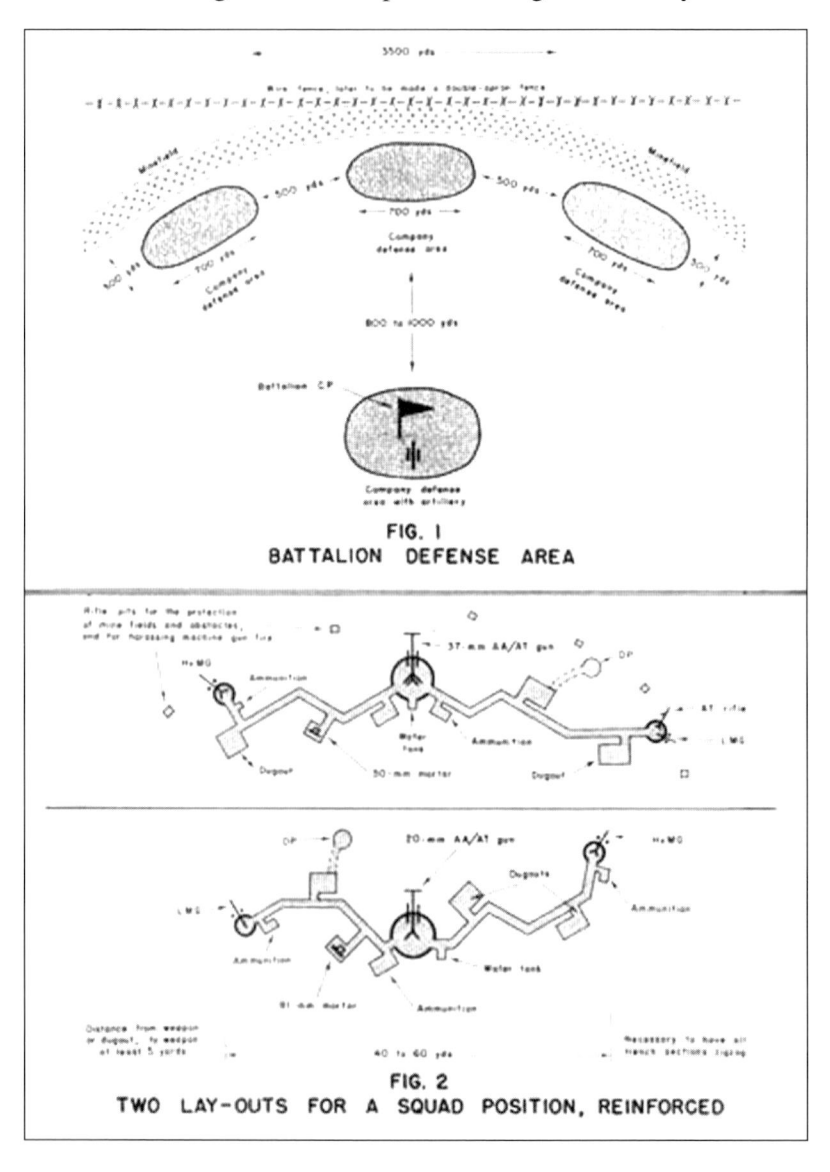

FIG. I
BATTALION DEFENSE AREA

FIG. 2
TWO LAY-OUTS FOR A SQUAD POSITION, REINFORCED

E. TRANSPORT

In rolling country, vehicles must be completely hidden from the view of the enemy. In level country, this result is obtained by keeping the vehicles well to the rear of the combat positions, and by using camouflage with nets. These nets can be improvised with open mesh wire covered with any sort of brush or camel thorn.

***

Comment: Figure 1 indicates in diagramatic form the lay-out for a battalion defense area on more or less level ground. In actual practice, of course, natural defense positions would be entrenched. The front-line wire, naturally, would scarcely be laid out in a straight line. Both diagrams are based on German sketches, and are notable for their simplicity.

The three forward company defense areas are composed of several platoon strong-points subdivided into squad positions like the ones illustrated in figure 2. The large number of heavy and automatic weapons is worth noting. A squad area provided with an AA/AT gun, a mortar, a Hv MG, a LMG all well dug in and mutually supporting, flanked by similar squad areas and reinforced with the fire of infantry cannon from the support position, make a defensive position of great power, entirely aside from the garrison's rifle and grenade fire. Such a defense area could, if necessary, be supplied from the air if ground communications were cut off.

By necessity, the plan here outlined bears a superficial similarity to defensive layouts found in our own field manuals, but it should be noted that the method prescribed in the above document is based on the German theory of defense against the principal effort in a German armored attack. Such an attack combines overwhelming local superiority in men and equipment, the onset of tanks with motorized infantry and artillery following, combined with a fire from massed artillery, mortar and heavy weapons of the utmost possible violence, supported

GERMAN PLATOON DEFENSE AREA

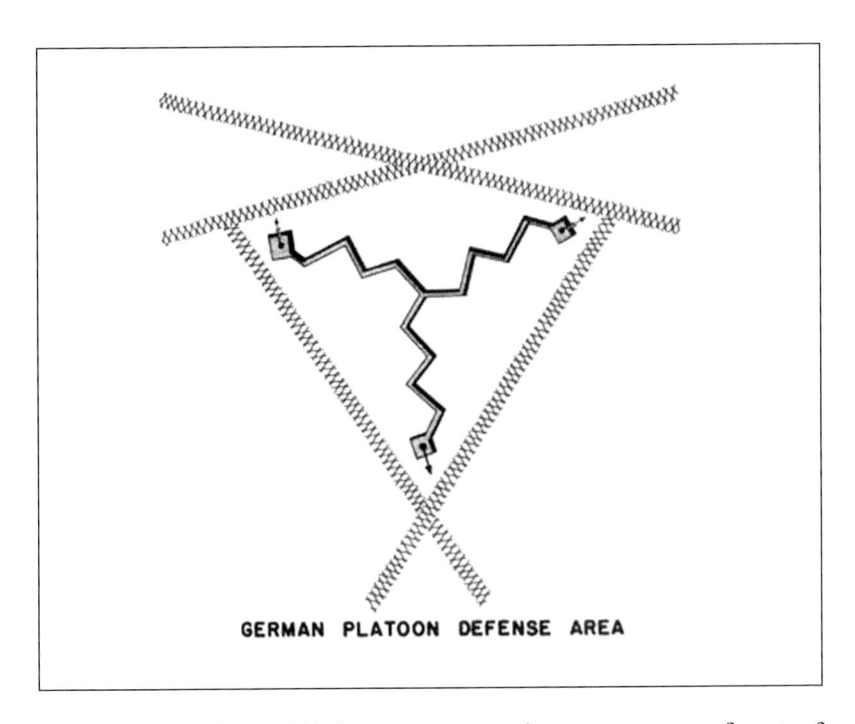

by dive-bombing. All is concentrated on a narrow front of perhaps 1,500 yards. The theory of defense assumes that the islands of resistance must allow the tanks to pass through since they can not prevent it, but do endeavor to stop by fire especially from the flank, the motorized infantry and artillery which follow behind. Cut off from their supporting infantry, the tanks are expected to be stopped by the rear elements of the defense and destroyed. A counterattack launched by the rear elements follows to eject any remaining enemy forces that retain a foothold in the defense system.

The extraordinarily wide frontage, 3,500 yards, is remarkable, as well as the wide spaces between the company defense areas - 500 yards. One commentator suggested that this defense would be far easier to pierce than our own more closely-knit system, but it must be remembered that the German plan here outlined is based on no theoretical study but upon the hardest possible school of African battle.

Another interesting feature is the concentration of heavy

weapons entirely within the company defense areas.

A third feature is in the extensive use of minefields. Whether these minefields are laid by the garrison or by engineers is not made clear in the instructions, but as each German infantry company contains a group of men trained to lay and lift mines, it seems reasonable to suppose that the minefield in front of the battalion area was to be laid by the garrison. The absence of any indication of mines between the company defense areas is rather odd. It would seem logical to mine these avenues rather heavily. The failure to indicate such mining should, however, not necessarily preclude the possibility that mines might be found there. The system here illustrated would appear vulnerable to infantry attack. This, in fact, was the method used by Montgomery at Alamein, where, reversing the German practice, infantry and engineers equipped with mine detectors led the assault, behind a devastating artillery barrage. It is understood, however, that the British had a substantial superiority in both guns and tanks.

In southern Tunisia was found a rather unusual lay-out for a German platoon on the defensive. American officers report that inside the wired-in company defense areas, were wired-in platoon defense areas, laid out in a more or less Y shape. The accompanying sketch is schematic, and not to any scale, but illustrates the plan of such a position.

One branch of the Y, or the broad angle might be pointed forward, or occasionally, one branch ran over a crest with the other two limbs on the reverse slope. Automatic weapons were placed at the ends of the trenches; the trenches themselves were sometimes blasted out of the rock. Mutually supporting crossfire, of course, was provided throughout the company area.

8. OBSERVATIONS ON GERMAN ARTILLERY TACTICS

A brief report by Allied observers on German artillery tactics in North Africa, from Tactical and Technical Trends, No. 31, August 12th, 1943.

A recently returned American officer reports that in North Africa the Germans frequently made a practice of firing a few salvoes from a battery; then, moving out, about the time the American forward observers had the position taped. Our own guns would plaster the observed position only to find that the enemy guns, apparently on self-propelled mounts, opened fire from some other point.

An extremely clever trick was reported to have been turned by a German tank unit upon which a British 25-pounder (88 mm) battery was attempting to adjust. After the first salvo hit at some distance from the tanks, a second was fired which apparently fell

A Fallschirmjäger motorcycle messenger passes a Tiger tank in Tunisia during 1943.

wide, and the third salvo went wider; the forward observer was frantic.

This is what had happened: the German tanks had timed the first salvo from the report to the instant of burst, which can be done with a low-velocity piece such as the 25-pounder, and fired a salvo from their own guns so that their own shells burst on the ground some distance away from the tanks at the same moment when the battery's shells struck. The forward observer was attempting to correct his own fire from German shell bursts.

The most dangerous German artillery fire was not from HE bursting on impact, but HE time fuze air bursts, and ricochet fire. In this latter type of shelling, the projectiles would strike the ground and ricochet upward, bursting over the heads of the troops.

A rather surprising percentage of the German shells were duds. Whether this was caused by defective fuzes, or for the reason that the projectiles were AP, used when the supply of HE had been exhausted, was not known.

9. ARMORED FORCE TACTICS IN THE MIDDLE EAST

An observer's report on German armored tactics in North Africa, from the Intelligence Bulletin, February 1943.

1. INTRODUCTION

United Nations observers in Libya have reported that there are four principles that German armored units seldom fail to consider before advancing to attack.

a. The primary role of the tank is to kill infantry.
b. The machine gun is therefore an important weapon of the tank.
c. The tank can be successful only when it is used in conjunction with all arms.
d. Tanks must be used in mass.

As a result of these views, the Germans will not fight a tank versus tank battle if they can avoid doing so. Moreover, their tactics are always based on having their armor move with other arms, in close support, in the form of a "box" or moving defense area.

2. THE BOX

The box is that part of the German column which appears inside the solid lines in figure 2. It varies in size, but if an armored battalion is the basic unit, the box might contain the following combat troops, in addition to tank ground crews and other service troops: 1 battalion of motorized infantry, usually carried in half-tracked, semi-armored vehicles; 1 battalion of 50-mm antitank guns; 1 battalion of 88-mm antiaircraft-antitank guns; 1 battalion of 150-mm close-support guns, sometimes on self-propelled mounts; and 1 battalion of divisional field artillery. Under these circumstances, the box would be approximately 2 miles deep, with a frontage of 200 yards.

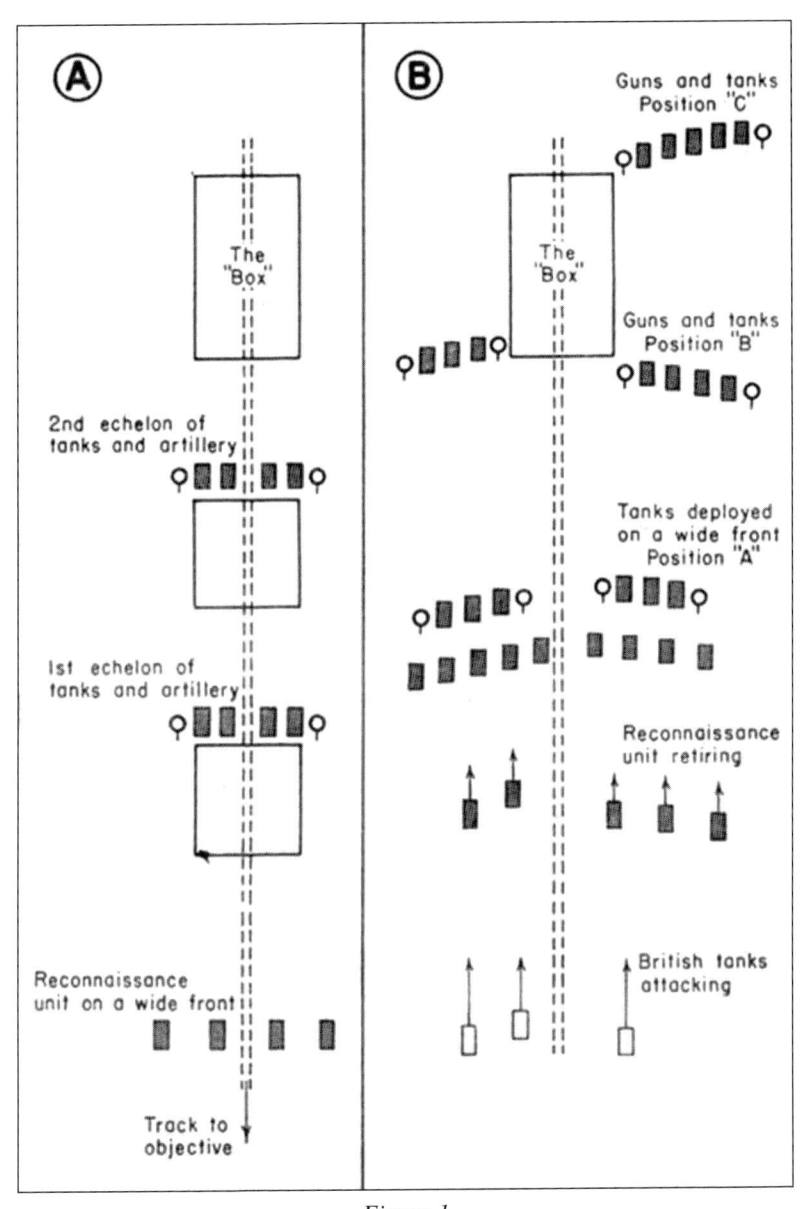

Figure 1

On the move or in the attack, the dispositions of the guns in the box are as shown in figure 2; that is, the antitank and antiaircraft guns guard the flanks and the front. The infantry guns and field guns usually are inside the box only when the defensive is assumed.

The 88-mm, although a very effective antitank gun, is included in the box primarily to protect the "soft-skinned" vehicles from air attack.

3. METHOD OF ADVANCE *(see fig. 1a)*

Over flat terrain the distances between the various elements of the German column are approximately as follows: between the reconnaissance unit and the first echelon of tanks, 5 to 10 miles; between the first and second echelons of tanks, 1 mile; and between the second echelon of tanks and the box, 2 miles. The whole formation is directed toward an objective which, if seized, will force the opposition to fight and thus become engaged on ground of German choosing.

On normal terrain each element of the German column moves from high ground to high ground, and the separate echelons of tanks are supported by field artillery, which moves behind them.

4. METHOD OF FIGHTING IF ATTACKED ON THE MOVE

As soon as United Nations troops are reported to be advancing and contact appears imminent, the box halts and takes up a position for all-around defense. This can be done very quickly because of the type of formation it uses while on the move. As the United Nations tanks advance, the German reconnaissance unit falls back, and the two echelons of German tanks deploy on a wide front, as illustrated in figure 1b, position "A."

If the United Nations troops continue to advance, the Germans retire to position "B," and force the opposition to attempt to break through one flank.

If the opposition attacks the German left flank, the troops on the left of the box at position "B" fall back to position "C." If the opposing tanks pursue, they not only are engaged frontally by the German tanks from position "C," but are caught in the flank by the antitank and antiaircraft guns protecting the left side of the box. The tanks of the German right flank at position "B"

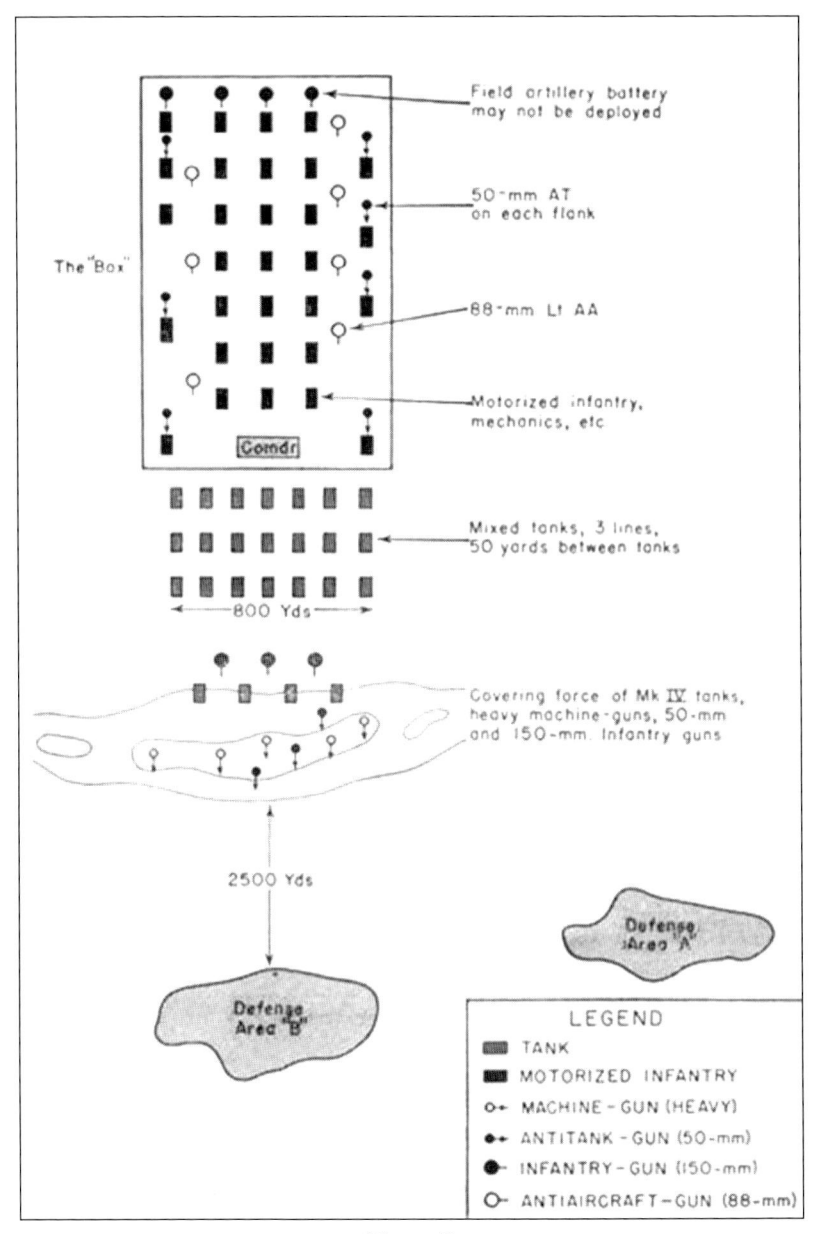

Figure 2.

then swing around and engage the attackers in the rear. If the artillery has accompanied the tanks in the advance, it may either continue to support them or may enter the box to increase its antitank strength.

5. ATTACK LED BY TANKS AGAINST A SINGLE DEFENSE AREA

The Germans realize that it usually is impossible for an attack in depth to pass between two defense areas or to cross the front of one defense area to attack another. The attack is therefore launched approximately "head on." Such an attack may be carried out in the following way:

a. Phase 1

The Germans will reinforce their reconnaissance unit with tanks deployed on a wide front, and will drive their covering force ahead until it is approximately 2,500 yards from the "crust" of the opposition's defense area (see fig. 2).

b. Phase 2

A most careful reconnaissance of the defender's positions will then be carried out by a senior commander in a tank, to decide which defense area to attack. In Libya last winter, when British defense areas were not necessarily sited on high ground, a great deal depended on whether the Germans could get a position about 2,000 yards from the British front on which to deploy the German covering force. In figure 2 it is assumed that the Germans found this, and are going to attack defense area "B."

c. Phase 3

The covering force now deploys as follows: Tanks, generally Mark IV's, take up a hull-down position on the ridge, and with the fire of their machine guns attempt to pin the defense. They may engage visible antitank guns with their 75-mm's. Under cover of this fire, 50-mm antitank guns, heavy machine guns, and close support 150-mm infantry guns are also deployed in an attempt to knock out the antitank guns of the defense or to kill their crews.

The majority of the weapons in the deployed covering force are dependent on direct laying and therefore can be blinded by smoke.

Under cover of the fire of their covering force, the Germans form their rear in the following manner:

(1) Three rows of tanks, with about 50 yards between tanks and about 150 yards between rows.

(2) When the tanks are in position, the box forms in the rear, as illustrated. The infantry ride in their carriers.

d. Phase 4

At zero hour the entire formation moves forward at about 15 miles per hour, depending on the terrain. As the tanks pass through their covering force, they begin to fire, not so much with a view to hitting anything as for psychological effect.

Arriving at defense area "B," some tanks drive straight through to the far side, while others assist the infantry in mopping up. The infantry usually do not dismount from their carriers until they arrive in defense area "B," when they fan out, using Tommy guns extensively.

e. Phase 5

If the attack is successful, the covering force moves forward into the captured area to stiffen the German defenses that are being established there. The tanks generally are withdrawn and serviced near what has now become the rear of the former defense area.

f. Conclusions

It takes 2 or 3 hours to prepare and stage such an attack.

If the attack proves successful, no minor counterattack is likely to drive the Germans out. Their defense is very rapidly organized, inasmuch as all the weapons they require are immediately available.

Such attacks are now being beaten off, and it is apparent that in the future they will not succeed without considerably increased artillery support.

The whole form of the attack has been reduced by the Germans to a "battle drill."

10. ENEMY ANTITANK MINE FIELDS AND BOOBY TRAPS IN AFRICA

The following is a report on an enemy minefield encountered by the British during the fighting tin Libya in late 1941.

All the mines were German Tellermines, which are antitank mines shaped like a plate and weighing about 11 pounds.

Many of these mines had pull-igniters screwed into the bottom as anti-lifting devices, and occasionally mines were laid upside down to increase the difficulty of disarming the main fuse. The mines were laid at very irregular intervals, but always on or near a desert trail. The mines laid across trails were generally marked with small piles of stones at the corners of the field. Mines were also laid along trails and these were apparently marked by piles of stones at either end of the mined section.

In some instances, places where mines were laid showed signs of the earth having been disturbed, but in others there was no such indication of mines because the ground had become smooth and sun-baked, owing to rain and sun.

Where trails ran through scrub, loose pieces of scrub, sometimes with booby traps attached, were placed on top of the mines as camouflage.

In several places a single strand of wire had been strung on tall stakes marked with warning or notice boards. These boards carry the inscription "ACHTUNG MINEN," or "ATTENTIONE MINA," or "ATTENTION MINES." The wire itself, although attached to booby traps, did not protect live minefields, which were invariably placed to one side of the wire, approximately in prolongation of it.

Dummy minefields were also encountered; these were completely wired in, and contained tins sunk into the ground

An interesting study of DAK troops on the move in March 1941. The pith helmets seen here were burdensome and uncomfortable and were soon discarded in favour of their cloth visored ski-caps.

with occasional booby traps attached to them. Gaps between dummy minefields were invariably sown with live mines.

A notice board with skull and cross bones painted on it always indicated booby traps. (This must not be taken to mean that all German booby traps are marked; the contrary is generally true.) These consisted of small standard charges ignited by standard German pull-igniters. The igniter may be attached by fine binding-wire to stakes in a wire fence, direct to the wire, to trip wires placed a few inches above ground, to stones which support stakes, or to the notice boards themselves. Booby traps also were generally laid in the scrub on either side of the trails. Occasionally a second booby trap was placed underneath the first to make the removal more difficult.

Booby traps could be detected by close scrutiny for anything out of the ordinary, i.e., notice boards facing, or in sight of, the enemy, loose strands of wire, sticks with wire wrapped round them, old explosive wrappings, etc. Stakes with booby traps underneath them were normally dug in, while others were driven in. White wood stakes protruding 6 inches above ground and connected by inconspicuous trip wires were sometimes found. These could usually be identified by the presence nearby of small excavations, containing explosive.

11. EMPLOYMENT OF ANTIAIRCRAFT FORCES WITH A GERMAN PANZER DIVISION IN LIBYA

The following report on German antiaircraft batteries with the 15th Panzer Division was originally published in Tactical and Technical Trends, No. 8, September 24th, 1942.

A captured order of the 15th Panzer Division of the Afrika Korps, dated May 25, 1942, affords an interesting example of the division commander's employment of the antiaircraft forces at his disposal. The order calls for the assembly of the 15th Panzer Division in an area 6 miles north of Rotunda Segnali (northwest of Bir Hacheim) in preparation for an attack. The attack actually began on May 26, and, it may be recalled, was the opening blow in Marshal Rommel's offensive which led to the capture of Tobruk and the Axis advance into Egypt to the El Alamein-Qattara Depression line. In forming for the attack the 15th Panzer Division occupied a central position, the 90th Light Division being on the right and the 21st Panzer Division on the left.

a. The 15th Panzer Division was organized for the attack as follows:

(1) Armored Group

The attack was headed by one tank battalion, immediately followed by the other tank battalion supported by a company of engineers and a light battalion of field artillery (twelve 105-mm howitzers).

(2) Reconnaissance Group

This group, which was employed to protect the right and open flank of the division's advance, was composed of the antitank battalion and the armored reconnaissance unit.

(3) Support Group

Composed of the medium battalion of the division artillery (twelve 150-mm howitzers) with a battery of 210-mm howitzers attached, the main divisional headquarters with supply and medical units, and the bulk of the engineers, this group advanced immediately behind the tanks.

(4) Infantry Group

Bringing up the rear were the motorized infantry regiment, supported by the other light battalion of field artillery, and the tank-recovery elements.

b. These antiaircraft forces were allocated by the division commander as follows:

Unit	Allocated to
(1) AA battalion staff	(1) AA battalion staff
(2) Heavy AA battery	Armored group. Prior to the commencement of the operation this heavy battery was ordered to protect the assembly against air attack.
(3) Light AA battery	
(a) Battery staff and 2 platoons (6 light guns)	Field artillery and engineers of the armored group.
(b) One platoon (3 light guns)	Field artillery of the support group.
(c) One platoon (3 light guns)	Heavy AA battery.
(4) Light AA battery less one platoon	
(a) Battery staff and 1 platoon (3 light guns)	AA battalion staff (in the support group).
(b) One platoon (3 light guns)	Engineers of the support group.
(c) One platoon (3 light guns)	Staff of 15th Pz Div.
(5) AA company (12 light guns)	
(a) Company staff and 2 platoons (8 light guns)	Motorized infantry group.
(b) One platoon (4 light guns)	Motorized infantry group.

c. The antiaircraft forces at the disposal of the division were as follows:

(1) Luftwaffe AA Units (part of the German Air Force)
(a) AA battalion staff.
(b) One heavy AA battery (six 88-mm guns and two 20-mm guns).
(c) One light AA battery (twelve 20-mm guns).
(d) One light AA battery less one platoon (nine 20-mm guns).

(2) Heeresflak Units (part of the Army, or ground forces)
One AA company (12 light guns).

(See this publication No. 7, page 7, for description of the distinction between Luftwaffe AA units, the main German antiaircraft arm, and Heeresflak units, which belong organically to the ground forces.)

d. The following points of interest arise from the above dispositions:

(1) Chain of command is from the AA battalion staff (attached to the staff of the division) through the heavy and light battery staffs with the armored group, and the light battery staff with the support group.

(2) The heavy battery is seen in a dual role. In the approach to battle it provides antiaircraft protection, turning to the ground role in support of the tanks when the battle starts.

(3) The light batteries protect the division and AA battalion staffs, the field artillery, the engineers, and the heavy AA battery against low-flying attack. The ground role is secondary.

(4) The AA company gives protection against low-flying attack to the motorized infantry and reconnaissance groups.

(5) The forces mentioned in the orders of the division do not comprise an entire antiaircraft battalion, the missing elements being two heavy batteries and one platoon of a light battery. This is significant as reinforcing the view, based on other information, that a considerable force of heavy antiaircraft guns (no doubt accompanied by a few light guns for close protection) was operating as an independent antitank group.

12. GERMAN SALVAGE PROCEDURE IN THE DESERT

The following intelligence report on German salvage of enemy equipment was originally published in Tactical and Technical Trends, No. 9, October 8th, 1942.

It has been stated that Marshal Rommel, in planning his campaigns, puts great emphasis on the capture of British equipment and supplies, and that the acquisition of large quantities of such booty has been one of the important factors in the success of his past operations in North Africa.

The importance of captured materiel in the German supply system is illustrated by a field order issued by Rommel on May 23, 3 days before the start of the German spring offensive. The order states: "The shortage of raw material and supplies in Africa makes it necessary to take every opportunity of seizing enemy

A British Matilda tank captured by the Afrika Korps in 1942 trundles across the Libyan desert under the flag of its new owners.

equipment and supplies. Units may take with them only such amount of captured materiel as will not impair their operational readiness; all other booty will be dealt with by a special Salvage Section (Beuteberge-Abteilung) of Panzer Army Headquarters.

"A guard is to be left over all dumps and stocks. The Salvage Section will make arrangements for the security and removal of all dumps and will provide technical personnel and transport. It is to be in direct communication with the forward troops. Captured supplies are to be marked in light blue paint with the words 'Tedesco' (Italian word for German) and 'Erfasste Beute' (captured booty). Strong disciplinary action is to be taken in the event of any misuse or destruction of salvage."

On several occasions during the course of the offensive, it was observed that, at the conclusion of an engagement, enemy salvage parties appeared on the battlefield and began recovery of transport and antitank guns before the evacuation of prisoners of war had been completed.

On the other hand, the Germans are equally thorough in measures taken to prevent their own materiel from falling in serviceable condition into British hands. For example, German vehicles used in the desert are equipped with demolition or incendiary bombs, and drivers are instructed to destroy their vehicles prior to capture. Similarly in a recent visit to the El Alamein battlefield, it was noted that captured Axis tanks, motor vehicles, artillery, and anti-tank guns in large numbers had been destroyed prior to capture.

13. OPERATIONS OF THE GERMAN TANK RECOVERY PLATOON

The following U.S. military report on German tank recovery during World War II was originally published in Tactical and Technical Trends, No. 12, November 19th, 1942.

British sources give recent information on the methods employed by the recovery platoon of (tank) workshop companies. This information was obtained from prisoners of war.

The towing vehicles and trailers of the platoon are sent forward to regimental headquarters and operate under its direction.

The principle now used is to have two or three recovery vehicles forward with the fighting units. These vehicles advance in the line of attack and cruise across the width of the battle front. The Germans believe that hostile forces will be preoccupied with the German tanks and will not bother with the recovery vehicles, no matter how close they are.

If a member of a tank crew orders the driver of a recovery vehicle to tow his tank to the rear, the former assumes responsibility for the action—in case it later proves that the damage is negligible and could have been fixed on the spot by the repair sections. However, asking that a damaged vehicle be towed away is always permissible if it is in danger of being shot up.

The towing vehicle usually goes forward alone and tows a disabled tank away by tow ropes. Towing is used in preference to loading on the trailer, as this latter operation may take 20 minutes (regarded by a prisoner as good time under battle

DAK officers pose for the camera in the ruins of Tobruk shortly after the capture of the port.

conditions).

The recovered tanks are towed to an assembly point behind the combat area, where they are lined up so as to protect themselves as far as possible. Trailers may be used to take back the disabled tanks from this point to the workshop company.

According to this report, however, trailers are being used less and less, and their use is confined mainly to roads. On roads, they enable a higher speed to be maintained, do not weave as much as a towed tank, and do not cut up the road surface. On the desert, trailers would be used on bad ground rather than where there is good going.

The PW's reported that drivers of recovery vehicles did front-line duty for about 8 days at a time; then they worked at the rear, between assembly point and workshop.

14. GERMAN TACTICS IN THE DESERT

The following intelligence report on German tank and antitank tactics in North Africa was originally published in Tactical and Technical Trends, No. 14, December 17th, 1942.

The support of tanks by the other arms is essential to success of tank operations. German application of this principle is illustrated in the following information on the Axis 1942 spring offensive in North Africa.

Great alertness was shown by the German forces in covering their front with antitank guns when their tanks were halted or stopped to refuel, and in protecting their flanks at all times with an antitank screen. A threat to the German flanks by tanks was immediately met by the deployment of antitank guns while the German tanks continued their movement. The enemy appears to have a rapid "follow the leader" system of deployment and a system of visual control by means of colored disk signals.

Allied prisoners being moved into captivity shortly after the fall of Tobruk.

A communications vehicle in operation, April 1942.

Every effort was invariably made to draw the fire of the defense, especially the fire of antitank weapons, by the deployment and advance of a few tanks. These tanks advanced, and were then withdrawn, and the enemy concentrated his artillery and mortars on all the defenders' weapons that had disclosed themselves. After a thorough preparation of this kind, the real tank attack was launched.

In at least one instance, a passage through a minefield was cleared for German tanks in this manner: A detachment of tanks advanced to the edge of the minefield and engaged all the defending weapons they could see. Pioneers then dismounted from the tanks and proceeded to clear mines on foot, covered by the fire of the tanks. Tanks that were hit were pulled out by other tanks and then replaced.

15. INITIAL ACTION ON THE EL ALAMEIN LINE

The following intelligence report on initial British attack at El Alamein was originally printed in Tactical and Technical Trends, No. 14, December 17th, 1942.

In the initial stages of the recent British offensive in Egypt, the 51st Highland and 9th Australian Divisions were assigned the mission of pushing a salient through the minefield in the northern sector of the El Alamein line, where the terrain is absolutely flat. After a penetration had been achieved, the British X Armored Corps was to move through and fan out in rear of the Axis positions. Because of the effective fire with which the Germans and Italians covered the minefield, most of the operations had to be conducted at night, and sufficient time allowed after completion to permit the infantry a minimum of 4 hours to dig in, construct their own fortifications, and prepare to resist any Axis counterattack.

The Australian division, which was in the extreme northern position, employed two regiments forward and one in reserve. The regiment on the right flank used one battalion forward on a front of 1,000 yards. In addition to the mission of attacking frontally, this battalion also had the task of securing the northern flank of the salient opened up by both the British divisions. The left flank regiment of the Australian division used two battalions forward and one in reserve, and coordinated its advance closely with the 51st Highland Division's right flank elements, which were immediately south of them.

The Australian division, operating on a 3,000-yard front, was heavily reinforced with artillery and was reported to have used 336 guns. Thirteen of these artillery regiments (probably about

300 guns) used 25-pounder weapons. In general, the preparation by the artillery was set to begin 20 minutes before H hour, and all guns were employed in counterbattery work for 15 of the 20 minutes. It is stated that in general the British employed their artillery on counterbattery missions at a ratio of 20 to 1 (presumably this means for all divisions at the front).

The tremendous artillery barrages were apparently extremely effective, and it is reported that for 2 hours after the initial attack was launched the German artillery was practically silent, unable to answer requests from their own infantry for defensive fire. Mention is made of attacks supported by a rolling barrage which was moved forward at a rate of 100 yards every 2 1/2 to 3 minutes, but it is not apparent whether this reference is to the British operations or to the heavy Axis counterattacks.

One observer in this theater believes that the tank has definitely been beaten by the antitank gun, and consequently the use of the tank in forward positions will be primarily strategical rather than tactical. He predicates this conclusion on the fact that the German 50-mm antitank gun and the British 6-pounder (57-mm) antitank gun, as well as higher calibers, can effectively disable any tank used today. The same observer also points out that mines have assumed major proportions in any defensive system, since infantry are prevented from making direct contact with the enemy until they have cleared and crossed intensive minefields swept by the defensive fire. Apparently, the British attack did not come as a surprise to the Germans, who expected it any time after October 14. The exact sector in which the main effort was to be made, however, was definitely not known to the Axis, and the British infantry thereby gained tactical although not strategic surprise.

16. GERMAN WIRE COMMUNICATION IN NORTH AFRICA

The following report on German communication in North Africa during World War II was originally published in Tactical and Technical Trends, No. 15, December 31st, 1942.

The following report was made after observation and inspection of the system of wire nets used by the Germans in North Africa.

A. GENERAL

The German use of wire communication is very flexible, and the extent of use varies according to the time available, conditions, and the tactical situation.

At periods when the troops are not engaged in active operations, a complete wire net is laid, and radio is used only by forward patrols and as an emergency means in case of interruptions and excess traffic over the wires.

Wire is not used as a means of communication during periods of inactive operations when mounted messengers are available. In forward areas, the Germans take every precaution against interruption of messages sent over the wire nets.

It is definitely known that in at least one German battalion, the orders issued to it specified that operational traffic was to be sent by telephone or telegraph until the latest possible moment: i.e., until the lines were cut by enemy action, and only then was radio to be used.

The following notes concern the wire network of the German Afrika Korps from June to October 1941. During this period there were no important operations; hence, what follows probably shows the fullest extent to which wire has been used in Africa by the Germans.

The Panzerjäger-Abteilung 39 (part of Kampfgruppe Gräf, part of the 21 Panzer Division) of the Afrika Korps on the move, 1942.

B. WIRE NETS

The wire nets for a large unit like the Afrika Korps may be divided into four classes.

(1) Local lines to the individual staff officers, corps headquarters, and communications personnel.

(2) Lines direct to lower units, corps troops, corps artillery etc., which are controlled directly by corps headquarters.

(3) Lines to the main units (divisions) under the command of the corps headquarters. These units themselves had large switchboards, through which corps headquarters could communicate directly with the regiments and battalions of the particular division.

(4) Lines to large centrals at fixed geographical points, such as Capuzzo, Gambut, and Gazala. These centrals were not in any unit headquarters, but provided a medium whereby corps headquarters could contact organizations not directly connected with it.

It must be noted, however, that there is no very clear distinction between (3) and (4) above. There are frequent instances of division switchboards acting as intermediaries between corps headquarters and non-corps divisions, or even of fixed centrals doing this, in addition to their normal function as the central exchange for their own regiments. Thus, in July and early August, the Trento Division switchboard carried the Afrika Korps communications to the Afrika Korps headquarters' switchboard at Gambut and Acroma, and to other Italian divisions such as the Brescia and Pavia (none of the Italian divisions belonged to the Afrika Korps.) In June, the Afrika Korps actually had no direct wire to the German divisions under its command. These were contacted through the Trento switchboard. Similarly, in September, the Bologna Division had nearly all the German heavy artillery units as subscribers, while at the same time the Afrika Korps headquarters' switchboard provided wire to the XXI Italian Army Corps, the Brescia and Littorio Divisions, and fixed centrals at Acroma and Gazala.

Furthermore, no distinction is made in the circuit diagrams between unit switchboards and fixed centrals.

Another interesting fact about the function of unit switchboards is that comparatively minor units frequently had more important units as subscribers. In August, for example, in the 15th Armored Division's wire net, the 1st Battalion, 33d Flak Regiment was the central for both the 15th Motorcycle Battalion and the 104th Motorized Infantry Regiment.

C. EXTENT OF AFRIKA KORPS WIRE COMMUNICATIONS

The comprehensive wire net developed after a period of static warfare can be shown by taking each of the four categories separately.

(1) Local Switchboard

In July there were some 21 lines from the Afrika Korps staff switchboard. The subscribers were either individual staff officers, or the officers of the various sections of the staff. Five or six additional lines were used for communications personnel (wire maintenance sections, etc.).

A DAK soldier equipped for the daily battle with the elements which made life a misery for the participants on both sides.

Heavy artillery in action on the Tunisian front, January 1943.

(2) Lines Direct to Corps Switchboards

The number of these lines varied according to circumstances. At one period in December, the Afrika Korps seems to have been acting as a fixed exchange for the Italian division at Bardia, and this involved a number of extra lines to installations and detachments. Normally, however, there were about six of these lines, and the units served were AA batteries protecting the headquarters, corps signal battalion, the intercept company, the air cooperation headquarters, and at some periods a reconnaissance unit and an airfield.

(3) Lines to Unit Switchboards

These lines again varied considerably. In June, 1941 the Afrika Korps had no direct lines to its own divisions. Instead, these were contacted through the Italian Trento Division. In October, there were direct lines to switchboards of all three German divisions, and the corps headquarters, while all Italians units were contacted through fixed centrals.

(4) Lines to Fixed Centrals

Early in the period the Trento Division acted as the most

important fixed central in the network, and the corps had direct lines also to central exchanges at Gazala and Acroma. During July and early August, the Trento Division and Capuzzo were the only centrals (apart from those of the German divisions) to which the Afrika Korps was directly linked. In mid-August the Bologna Division took over the complete role of the Trento Division. But in September and October, Afrika Korps had direct lines to two fixed centrals, Gambut and Capuzzo, which acted as intermediaries to all units not on the German division exchanges. These centrals correspond with the "North" and "South" sectors into which the Germans divided their main defensive area.

In the final stage of development of this network, after 3 months of position warfare, Afrika Korps had local lines for its various staff sections and staff officers, direct lines to six or seven corps troops units, lines to the switchboard of the corps headquarters, and of all three German divisions, whence lower echelons and units could be called, and finally lines to two large fixed centrals at Gambut and Capuzzo through which they could contact the main Italian units, smaller fixed exchanges, and other German units not covered by the corps wire net.

d. Divisional Wire System

A similar development is shown by the circuit diagram of the 15th Armored Division for the same period. There was a staff switchboard with up to 20 lines: direct lines to small units (AA, communication, medical companies, etc.); lines to main units, whence smaller organic units could be contacted; and lines to main exchanges like the Afrika Korps, or to Gambut for rear and lateral communications.

e. Subsequent Examples

Another circuit diagram showing the communications of the 155th Light Infantry Regiment from April 20, 1942 is interesting as an example of the German wire system.

The Afrika Korps had moved shortly before the date

mentioned above, and from the new position had communications only with the 15th Armored Division, 109th Motorized Infantry Regiment, and an Italian division. The old switchboard had not been moved, and was connected to the new one through a fixed central. This central and the old corps switchboard together provided the new installation with a means of communicating to the 21st Armored Division and other units.

The 90th Light Division, the unit to which the 155th Light Infantry Regiment was attached, had communication to the rear only to the XXI Italian Army Corps, to which command it was at this time attached. No lines to the front were shown from the 90th Division, and a radio net including the 155th Light Infantry Regiment is shown on this circuit diagram.

The 155th Light Infantry Regiment was amply supplied with forward wire lines, but had none to the rear except indirectly via a battery of the 611th Antiaircraft Battalion to the 104th Motorized Infantry Regiment, and thence to the Afrika Korps. The 155th Light Infantry Regiment had the following wire circuits:

(1) A staff switchboard with lines for the regimental commander, adjutant, signal detachment, observation post, etc;
(2) Lines from the switchboard terminating at telephones to the supporting artillery troops and antitank units;
(3) Lines to switchboards running to the two battalions of the regiment simplexed for telegraph.

The battalions had their own local staff lines and lines direct to company headquarters.

f. Forward Wire Communications - Infantry Battalion

Two circuit diagrams of the 1st Battalion, 115th Motorized Infantry Regiment, dated May 27 and June 16, 1941, respectively, show the wire net of an infantry battalion in the front line in Libya.

The earlier diagram shows rear and lateral lines from battalion headquarters to regimental headquarters, a neighboring battalion, and an artillery battery. On the later diagram there is an additional line to the 2d Battalion, 115th Motorized Infantry Regiment. On both dates, the line to regimental headquarters was simplexed for telegraph.

Communications within the battalion were, at the earlier date, as follows: lines from battalion headquarters to 1 and 3 Companies, and radio communication to 2 Company. Both 1 and 3 Companies had lines to 2 Company, and each company had a line to an attached mortar Or machine-gun section. In addition, battalion headquarters had lines to two observation posts manned by elements of the heavy weapons company, and from one of these, there was a line to a platoon of the cannon company.

By June 16, the three companies had been compressed to two, a "Left" Company and a "Right" Company, each with one platoon in front. Lines to platoons and sections of the heavy weapons company no longer went back from company headquarters, but forward from rear observation posts, and an additional line was provided from battalion headquarters to an engineer platoon. The radio net from battalion headquarters to 2 Company was no longer shown.

The 33d Artillery Regiment's wire communications were shown in a circuit diagram to be as follows:

(1) A switchboard with a line back to division headquarters, and local lines to the staff officers;

(2) A second switchboard with lines to each of the three battalions and to the observation posts.

Radio was used for communication between command vehicles of the regiment, and the battalion commanders and observation officers in tank-supporting artillery units; wire cannot be used for these purposes.

17. GERMAN ATTACK AT EL ALAMEIN

The following report on the German attack at El Alamein in 1942 was originally printed in Tactical and Technical Trends, No. 17, January 28th, 1943.

AUGUST 31-SEPTEMBER 5, 1942

INTRODUCTION

After the British attempt to penetrate Rommel's lines on July 27, 1942 had failed, the Egyptian front settled into a more or less stagnant period for a few weeks. During this period, outside of the constant artillery fire, night patrolling, and usual air activity, little in the nature of active military operations took place. Most of this time was utilized by both sides in preparing defensive positions and building up strength in personnel, equipment, and supplies.

During the month of August the British reached a new high in morale. This change in attitude was attributed by observers to three main factors. First, the complete turnover which had taken place in the supreme command. General Alexander, a World War I veteran, noted for his aggressiveness and the leader of two brilliant actions of World War II, had replaced General Auchinleck as High Commander in the Middle East. Now under Alexander and in direct command of the British Eighth Army, was Lieutenant General Montgomery, a veteran of the fighting in France in World War II, and a soldier's soldier. Second, the quantity and quality of rations, which in the past had left much to be desired, had increased to a point where the British Tommy was not the underfed and under-nourished soldier that Rommel's troops had previously faced. Third, the British had gained a much-needed and well-deserved rest.

British Crusader tank passes a burning German Panzer IV tank during Operation Crusader.

The British, in particular, were very thorough in their plans for the anticipated battle with Rommel's forces. About the middle of August it became evident, from the nature of the position that the British were taking, that they did not intend to attack, but instead that their strategy was based on the fact that Rommel could and would. With this thought in mind, the British prepared their position for defensive action only. By restricting themselves in this fashion, the British hoped to be able to keep their armor from falling into antitank ambush, similar to that which had caused their defeat a few weeks earlier. Since they planned to remain on the defensive, the British were also able to site their guns so as to have immediate antitank and artillery support, which had been lacking in the earlier attack.

After the British command had committed themselves to the defensive, they spared neither time nor labor to make certain that no possible contingency could arise which would frustrate them. Every man had been instilled with the feeling that he, and he alone, might mean the difference between victory and defeat. The line that they would be defending was commonly known as "Egypt's Last Hope"; with its fall, Egypt was lost. During the period from the June 27 attack to the latter part of August, every conceivable defensive position had been tested all along the entire line. Terrain exercises and maneuvers were going on constantly, testing and improving the defenses. All tanks had been moved in and out of pre-selected battle positions, actually dug in, and placed in hull-down and gun-down positions. All drivers and all gun crews were thoroughly familiar with their duties and positions. Likely targets had been registered upon, and gun and tank crews had gone to their positions in darkness.

GERMAN PLANS

Of Rommel's general plan little is known. It is known that he was preparing a strong position and his armored strength increased in tanks, both German and Italian. German and Italian parachute troops made their appearance on this front, as well as elements of the German 164th Division. Despite continual bombings by British and American planes, the port facilities at Benghasi, Tobruk, and Matruh were still open, and through them, some supplies still reached the forward elements. The railroad from Tobruk to Daba also remained open, although traffic was severely hindered by the continual bombing by Allied planes.

Allied air reconnaissance showed that Rommel was regrouping his forces, with a large part of the German and Italian infantry, and the Italian armor, identified on the southern flank of his line, and with the bulk of the German armor behind the center although in a position to join overnight a thrust on the south.

About August 25, the Axis air force began to build up its strength in serviceable planes.

BRITISH PLANS

The British general plan was to prepare several contiguous fortified areas along the coast and to hold them at all costs, and also to cover the high ground of Ruweisat Ridge and the ridge immediately south of it. They also planned to hold the New Zealand "box" covering the western edge of Deir El Hima. The armor was to take up defensive positions along the foot of Alam El Haifa escarpment and maintain this position, thereby intending to force the German armor to fight them on ground chosen by the British. The southern sector was to be defended by two parallel mined areas extending to Himeimat, which is along the edge of the Qattara Depression. The bulk of the British armor was to be held in the south-central sector and well behind the minefields. In support of the infantry defending the fortified areas was an armored brigade (British brigade approximates U.S. regiment). Portions of the light armor and elements of the motor brigade patrolled and guarded the minefields. The light armor on the south would harass any advance, and the armored reserve (another armored brigade) was to be held in readiness to the east.

In the absence of any specified missions, the Royal Air Force, combined with the American Air Force, was to bomb continually and strafe the Axis ports, supply lines, and troop concentrations day and night.

British Intelligence fully expected the Axis offensive to get underway during the full moon on the night of August 25/26. For some reason, said by some to be a lack of fuel, the attack did not materialize at this time. However, on the night of August 30/31, just prior to midnight, Rommel launched the long-expected attack which he hoped would bring him victory, and drive the British from North Africa.

OPERATIONS: AUGUST 31

Rommel's attack on the strongly prepared British El Alamein line commenced at 2320, August 30. At that time German

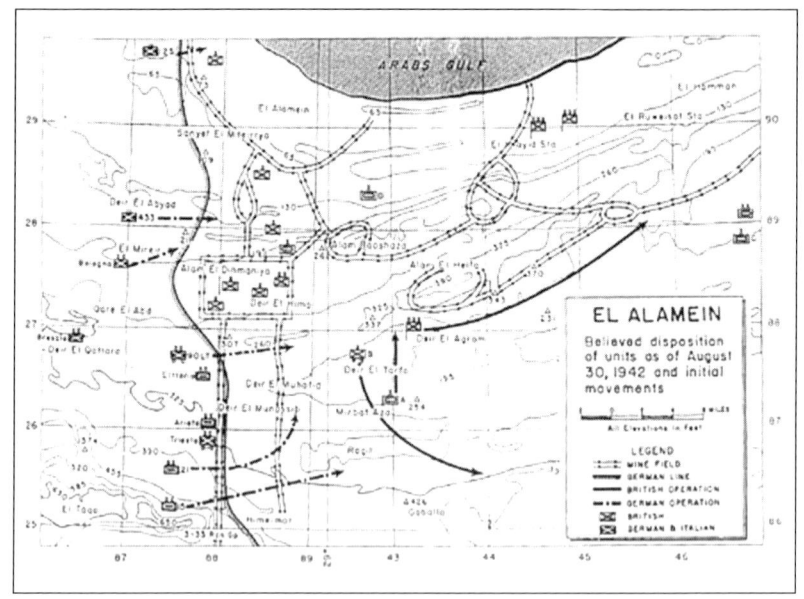

El Alamein - Initial disposition and movements

engineers and infantrymen commenced clearing a passage through the western section of the British minefield between the 25th and 26th east-west grid lines in the vicinity of Himeimat.

An interesting sidelight on this preliminary operation, and the subsequent tank penetration, was that the British fully intended to shell the Axis armor while they were confined and restricted in movement during passage through the minefield, but due to a misinterpretation of orders, this was only lightly done. As a result the Axis tanks managed to get through the minefields comparatively unharmed.

The German 15th Armored Division, with approximately 140 tanks, came through the minefield just north of Himeimat practically unharmed, then turned due east. Around noon they were in the vicinity of the 43rd north-south grid. At this point, for some reason not fully understood, they halted their advance, and formed up as though they were expecting a counterattack. When the expected counterattack did not materialize, they formed up in the area east of Deir el Ragil, and proceeded in a northeasterly direction at about 1600. At the same time they detached about 40 tanks, which remained in the area of Deir el Ragil as security for the southern flank. It appeared that the German armor would bypass the principal British position, and, in order to prevent this, and to draw the Germans northward, the British commander sent a detachment composed of two tank battalions south to make contact, and, if possible, draw the Axis tanks north. This move was successful, as the British detachment returned to its previous position closely followed by the 15th Armored Division. A patrol of the 15th Armored Division closed in on the left flank of British Armored Brigade "A"* defending the main position on the southern side of Alam El Halfa, and a short engagement followed. After dark the 15th Armored withdrew to the south, leaving about 13 tanks behind in a wrecked or burning condition.

The German 21st Armored Division crossed the minefield with the 15th Armored, then turned in a northeasterly direction. It reached the area north of Deir el Tarfa at 1700. At this point it came under the fire of the right flank of British Armored Brigade "A" southwest of point 337. As the Axis tanks closed in, a brisk fight followed which lasted till dark. The 21st Armored then withdrew to the vicinity of point 254, leaving approximately 15 tanks burning or totally destroyed.

The German 90th Light Infantry Division which was on the north flank of Rommel's southern group, had difficulty in crossing the minefields, but by evening had succeeded in reaching the area north of Deir el Muhafid.

South of the 90th Light were the Italian divisions, Littorio, Ariete, and Trieste, in the area Deir El Munassib. Of these latter three outfits, only the Trieste completely crossed the minefields during the engagement.

German Reconnaissance Groups 3 and 33 advanced east, and then turned south towards the area Qua El Labin.

In the central sector a localized Axis thrust by the German 433rd Infantry Regiment and the Italian Bologna Division

Panzer III of the 10th Panzer Division in Tunisia 1943.

against the Indian outfits (aided by the South African and the New Zealand brigades) on Ruweisat Ridge, advanced as far as point 211, but was later driven back by counterattack.

In the northern sector, another localized Axis attack by the German 125th Infantry Regiment was momentarily successful near Tel el Eisa, but was later driven hack to its original position by the Australian brigade occupying that sector.

Patrols of British Motor Brigade "B" were active in the east and also in the Himeimat area. The remainder of the British Eighth Army held to their defensive positions, and only fought that part of the Axis forces that attacked them. Allied air support was continuous and intensive, as was the British artillery support, given from the area near Alam el Halfa where it was concentrated.

In a review of the day's fighting, two points stand out. First, the Axis attack did not come as a surprise to the British. Second, the British held rigidly to their preconceived defensive plan. They did not counterattack but waited, as planned, and met the Axis tanks on ground of the British choice.

During the night of August 31/September 1, British Armored

Brigade "C", then in reserve, was ordered to advance and tie in with the left flank of Armored Brigade "A" to form a line along the foot of the Alam el Haifa escarpment.

OPERATIONS: SEPTEMBER 1

Just prior to daylight, the Axis tanks formed for the attack. The 21st Armored Division with approximately 50 tanks was along Deir el Agram facing the center of the main British position.

The 15th Armored Division, with about 100 tanks, formed southeast of the left flank of Armored Brigade "A".

At daylight, severe fighting broke out and continued until 1100. During the first hour of the fight, Armored Brigade "C" fought forward from its position in reserve, made contact with the left flank of Armored Brigade "A" on the main position, and formed as directed. This advance by the British armored reserve prevented the envelopment of the left flank of the principal British force.

It should be pointed out that the Armored Brigade "C" had been ordered to the position it eventually took during the previous night. However, the orders were not received until late at night, and execution was not as rapid as was expected.

The engagement was resumed in the late afternoon and continued until dark when the Axis withdrew to point 254 ridge, leaving behind 25 burning or totally destroyed tanks.

During the day a third Armored Brigade "D" went into position between the right flank of Armored Brigade "A" and the New Zealand box.

OPERATIONS: SEPTEMBER 2

During the night, the Axis formed up along the ridge at point 254, on the defensive behind a screen of antitank guns.

After daylight, small and isolated groups of Axis tanks felt out positions occupied by Armored Brigade "D" which had been moved up the previous day, but no attack developed.

The 90th Light Infantry Division commenced withdrawing

from its position east of the minefield. It was replaced by the Trieste, supported by the Ariete and Littorio. The Italian Brescia Division moved forward from the area Deir El Munassib, and took up a position facing the southwest corner of the New Zealand box.

Allied bombing and artillery fire was continuous and heavy, both by day and night. Armored car patrols had gone around the Axis line and were harassing Axis supply lines far to the rear.

OPERATIONS SEPTEMBER 3

The day of September 3 was comparatively quiet. Axis motor transport commenced withdrawing westward along its axis of advance.

During the day British light armor, and patrols from Motor Brigade "B" intensified their harassing activities from the east and south as far west as Himeimat.

Artillery elements joined these patrols and shelled the Axis motor transport from comparatively close-up positions, then withdrew in face of enemy pressure.

The British heavy armor remained in place along Alam el Halfa.

It appeared at this time that Rommel was still undetermined as to his course of action. He had failed to draw the British armor away from its support, or into antitank ambush; in fact, the British failed to play the game the way he wanted them to play it.

OPERATIONS: SEPTEMBER 4

During the early morning hours, the New Zealand Division, composed of the two New Zealand brigades, which occupied the box, assisted by a brigade of another infantry division, laid down an artillery barrage and followed with an infantry attack. This attack advanced south and along the trails in square 88-27.

The attack advanced 3 miles, but with the coming of daylight the Trieste, Brescia, and the 90th Light Division, supported by the Ariete, and Littorio Divisions, in a series of three counterattacks, forced the attacking troops back nearly to their original positions.

This effort served one great purpose, however, in that it was evidently the deciding factor in causing Rommel's withdrawal. The force of this attack prevented him from using the 90th Light in a coordinated attack with the German armor.

The air and artillery attacks were continued on the same large scale as heretofore.

OPERATIONS: SEPTEMBER 5

The bulk of the Axis transport was withdrawn west of the minefields. The 90th Light withdrew off to the west. An antitank screen, supported by tanks, was set up between Himeimat and Deir el Munassib.

This was a slow withdrawal, with Rommel utilizing to the full extent his old scheme of leaving tanks visible as bait for British armor. These tanks were well protected by antitank guns. Formerly the British had always pursued them, and frequently had lost rather heavily. This time, all British armored forces remained in their battle positions, with their artillery continually firing on the retreating Axis forces.

Whenever the pursuing British infantry gun-carriers came within range, the Axis antitank guns picked them off. Rommel withdrew carefully, sustained only a minimum of losses, and eventually halted very close to his original position, retaining only about 2 miles of the ground he had won on the first day.

The Axis line in the southern sector was formed by the Italian Brescia and Trieste Divisions in the northeast part of square 87-26. The Ariete Division was at Deir el Munassib. The 90th Light Division was about 7 miles to the rear of the Ariete, as a mobile reserve. The German 21st Armored Division, the 3 and 33 Reconnaissance Groups, and the Italian Littorio Division covered the area around Himeimat and west to El Taqa.

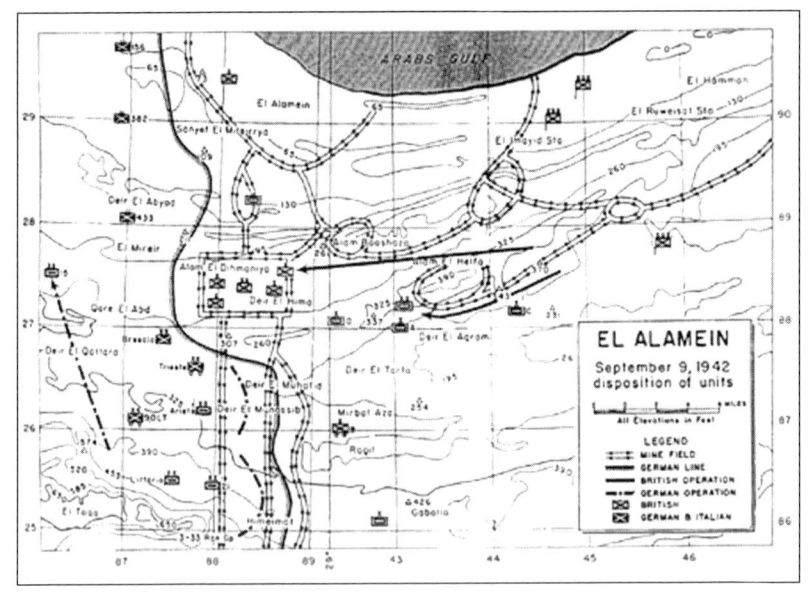

El Alamein - Final Disposition

While the Axis motor transport was retreating through the minefield area, the Axis air force managed to put up a fighter covering force which prevented Allied bombings. This protective covering "umbrella" was only local, however, and Allied bombing of the Axis rear areas continued on an undiminished scale.

When Rommel took up the position mentioned above, he immediately prepared strong defenses, and the El Alamein battle of August 1942 was at an end.

LOSSES

The Axis withdrawal was orderly, and since none of the previous engagements had been on a large scale, the loss of equipment throughout the entire battle was not unduly large.

Observers estimate that the Axis lost not more than 70 of their total of 440 tanks; of those lost, 55 were German.

Approximately 100 Axis motor transport vehicles, of which the majority were captured British vehicles, were destroyed and left on the field.

Judging from the empty cans lying about the areas that the

Axis troops had occupied and then given up, the Axis forces appeared to be completely rationed with previously captured British supplies.

The British entered the battle with a grand total of 546 tanks of all types, and lost or had disabled a total of 67 tanks, which included British mediums and American medium and light M-3's. Of the total number of tanks lost, it was estimated that not more than 20 were completely destroyed and beyond repair.

British personnel losses were relatively light. A British corps commander estimated that the Axis losses were greater than the British in a proportion of 2 to 1.

SUMMARY

Rommel first advanced with his entire striking force, but there was no indication that a full-fledged, all-out assault had been launched. It is believed that he hoped to engage the British armor on grounds of his own choice, defeat it and then occupy Ruweisat Ridge which commands the coast road and the avenue to Alexandria.

When the British tanks refused to come out of their hull-down defensive positions, and away from their antitank and artillery support, Rommel was not quite sure of his ground and was afraid to risk his full strength. He spent 2 days feeling out the British position, losing rather heavily in tanks and motor transport while doing so. In view of later developments, it is also believed that he underestimated British tank strength.

Rommel was not able to bypass the principal British position along Alam El Haifa and then proceed eastwards to the Delta (El Hamman) because of the constant danger to his supply line by the British armor, plus the constant interference from Allied bombing and artillery.

On realizing the full extent of the British strength, Rommel withdrew to his previous line and occupied the strongest defensive position in the Western Desert.

The British success was due to: security; the well-planned defense which had been thoroughly tested by many tactical exercises; a thorough knowledge among troops and unit commanders of what was expected; proper execution and coordination among higher echelons; and the continual artillery and air bombardments. The effect of these bombardments, while not producing great material damage, must be accounted as a decisive factor.

In the employment of armament the most outstanding points were: the British static use of tanks; the effect of antitank guns; and complete utilization of field artillery mobility.

The only notable achievement of the German Luftwaffe was their ability to maintain a protective fighter-umbrella for several hours during the withdrawal of motor transport through the minefields, despite over-all Allied air superiority.

18. ENEMY MINEFIELDS AT EL ALAMEIN

The following U.S. military report on German and Italian minefields at El Alamein was originally printed in Tactical and Technical Trends, No. 19, February 25th, 1943.

Information concerning the type, layout, and marking of enemy minefields in the El Alamein area has become available from British sources. There is as yet no information as to whether this general method of mine laying was also followed in the Axis retreat from El Alamein.

A. PATTERN AND SPACING

The minefields were laid in belts, each belt consisting of two to eight rows of mines. Shallow minefields might have only a single belt of mines consisting of from two to four rows; deep fields might have several belts of mines with considerable distance between belts.

The belts themselves might be anything up to 200 yards deep, with an additional danger area consisting of widely scattered mines up to 250 yards in front of the belt. The back of the belt was usually marked with a fence; the distance from this fence to the front fence (if any existed) was anywhere from 100 to 800 yards.

No standard pattern for laying mines in the belts appeared to be used. However, from the mass of data that was available, it was found possible to classify the patterns broadly as follows:

(1) Regular Pattern

This is the most common. Mines in a given row are spaced at equal distances; there is an equal distance between rows; and the mines of one row are equally spaced between the mines of the previous row. A variation in this method is to vary the distances between rows. In no reported case, except for scattered mines, has the distance between mines in a row been unequal.

(2) Regular Pattern Offset

By a system of pacing, a certain variety is introduced into the regular pattern. The distance between mines in any one row is equal, but one row is slightly offset from the previous row, and the next row is again offset by a different distance. Once a few mines have been located, the pattern soon becomes apparent and mines will be found where expected.

(3) Random Mines

In front of most regular minefield belts, and particularly in front of gaps, there may be found mines scattered at random and unmarked. These are either continuous, with very wide and irregular spacing, or in clumps more closely spaced but laid to no pattern inside each clump.

The above patterns usually resulted in a density of a little less than 1 mine per yard of front. Densities up to 2 mines per yard were generally not found except when blocking roads, trails, or defiles.

The spacing between the mines in a given row is from 3 to 10 yards, with the average spacing being 6 yards. As noted in (1) above, in no reported case, except for scattered mines, has the distance between mines in a row been unequal.

The most common spacing between the rows themselves is reported to be usually about 5 yards or 10 yards.

B. MARKING OF FIELD

The front edge of forward minefields is often not marked. The rear edge normally is marked, usually with a trip wire on short stakes, though cattle-fence, concertina wire, and stone cairns are sometimes used. Cases have been reported of the rear edge being unmarked.

A common marking is a single row of concertina wire running along the center of a field parallel to the rows of mines. in a large minefield there may be several rows of mines in front unmarked, then a row of concertina wire, more mines, then concertina wire, and so on, finishing up with a row of concertina

Rommel at work in his command half-track during June 1942.

wire on the rear edge.

The marking of fields by furrows, commonly used at Tobruk, has only once been reported at El Alamein, and in that case the field was a dummy one.

Only one case has been reported of continuous wire running irregularly within a field. It is believed that skull and crossbones indicate the presence of antitank mines or booby traps.

In the rear areas, enemy minefields may be expected to be well marked with cattle-fences and warning notices in German and/or Italian.

C. MARKING OF GAPS

Little information is available about gaps through minefield; but the following data have been reported.

(1) Width

10 yards in one case, and in another.

(2) Method of Closing

Usually two or three rows of Tellermines (antitank) with boards placed on one or all of the rows to insure detonation of mines if a vehicle attempts to pass through the gap over the boards, which are normally concealed by a shallow cover of soil.

(3) Marking

In the northern sector, two types of gap markers have been found:
(a) Painted signs, as in sketch, on either side of the gap.
(b) Luminous tubes 1 inch long placed on the tops of mines to mark a route for patrols. These tubes are visible 3 yards away.

(4) General

It is reported that gaps are a favorite place for laying Tellermines without any marking wire or signs. Gaps are sometimes covered by groups of scattered mines laid up to 2,000 yards in front of the gap, and unmarked.

D. TYPES OF MINES

German, Italian, French, and British mines were all used by the enemy at El Alamein. Relatively few booby traps were found in

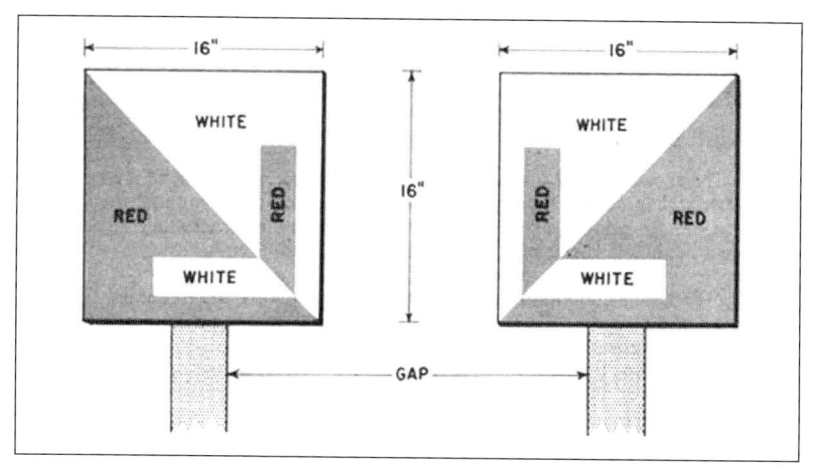

German minefield marker

the minefields, and the traps found were almost invariably attached to German Tellermines. Antipersonnel mines (usually Italian B4's) were found at times, generally as a single row laid in front of the outer wire of a minefield. The antipersonnel mines were spaced from 7 to 10 yards apart, with wooden pegs driven between the mines, these pegs being used to attach the trip wiring from the mines on each side of the pegs.

E. TACTICAL SITING

One report states that the minefield is usually 200 to 300 yards in front of the MLR, and covered by fire and listening posts. In another report the distance from the MLR to the main minefield is given as varying from 200 to 1,000 yards. A listening post was also located by a patrol 100 to 150 yards behind a minefield. It can be definitely stated that it is the enemy's practice by day to cover all main minefields with small-arms fire from close range, and by night to maintain antilifting patrols, as well as listening posts often located within the minefield itself.

Comment: It should be realized that the above information applies to the enemy mine tactics at El Alamein. It is to be expected that his tactics will change from time to time as a result of experience, expediency, change in terrain, or change in command personnel.

19. AXIS MOTOR VEHICLES IN NORTH AFRICA

The following military report on German and Italian military vehicles in North Africa was originally printed in Tactical and Technical Trends, No. 20, March 11th, 1943.

Representatives of a well-known Canadian motor vehicle manufacturer recently inspected enemy vehicles captured by the British in North Africa. The vehicles examined were German Ford and Opel-Blitz trucks, and Italian Spa trucks, varying from 1 1/2 to 8 tons. While the vehicles in question were not recent models, the following observations by the manufacturing representatives are of interest.

The front and rear springs of the vehicles inspected were heavily built. The leaves were wide and long. All front springs were equipped with two rebound leaves mounted on top of the spring. The first rebound leaf was three-quarters the length of the main leaf, and the top leaf was half the length of the main leaf. There appeared to be no broken springs on any of these vehicles.

The large diameter of the gasoline-filler neck greatly assists in refueling from small cans in the field. The gasoline tanks were enamel-plated on the inside to prevent rusting. The spare gasoline cans were similar to the American 5-gallon can, except that they were enamel-plated on the inside and that the neck was equipped with an attached, snap-on top instead of the threaded type.

Nearly all vehicles were equipped with oil-bath air cleaners. There were two types: one using a single metal-screen cone, and the other a double metal air cone, immersed in cylinder oil. The double unit takes in air over the top, but cleans the air twice

Afrika Korps soldiers drawing rations during April 1941. The high laced boots worn in this picture were soon discarded for a low cut boot similar to the British issue.

through two conical metal screens, one inside the other, with an air space between them. The single unit takes air in from the bottom, and the air is cleaned once through a conical metal screen. The representatives were much impressed with these air cleaners.

Practically all radiators were built of tubular removable sections, and this feature would assist considerably in repairing radiator cores.

20. GERMAN PATROLS IN NORTH AFRICA

The following report on German patrols in North Africa near El Alamein was printed in Tactical and Technical Trends, No. 22, April 8th, 1943.

The following items of information on certain German patrols in the El Alamein area have been obtained.

The patrols in question occurred at regular intervals of 4 days, the men being drawn from the various platoons in the company. At no time was a complete squad or platoon as such detailed for a patrol. One patrol consisted of 16 to 18 men under a platoon commander. The men were formed into two squads, and only the squad leaders were told the plans for the patrol. They left their main line of resistance and went out 1,500 to 2,000 yards in front of their minefields, in single file. Five or six men stayed behind to guard the gap through the minefield.

On another patrol, the covering party consisted of an NCO and six men armed with one machine gun, one Tommy gun, and hand grenades. A third patrol consisted of the equivalent of two platoons under the command of a company commander.

Neither telephone nor portable radio set was taken on these patrols, and no artillery officer accompanied them.

21. GERMAN AIR SUPPORT OF TANKS IN AFRICA

A report on Luftwaffe air support for armored units in North Africa, from Tactical and Technical Trends, No. 24, May 6th, 1943.

GAF air commands normally detail air liaison officers (Fliegerverbindungsoffiziere, or "Flivos") to the headquarters of Army divisions and higher units, to ensure that army requests for air support and air reconnaissance are properly transmitted to the air headquarters concerned.

However, the experience in the Libyan campaigns indicated that properly coordinated air support of armored units required the assignment of a GAF officer to armored combat echelons below division headquarters. Such an officer must be an experienced pilot, capable of rapidly estimating the weight of air attack necessary to support a particular field operation, and capable of directing the concentration of this attack on any given target at the moment which the tank commander determines to be most advantageous.

In this way, air strength can be utilized to its maximum effectiveness, avoiding the dispatch of large formations to deal with small targets or of insufficient numbers to cover large and scattered objectives. During an attack against a moving target, a liaison officer with flying experience can best direct the aircraft. He controls them by radio from a vantage point where he can watch, and if necessary, follow up the target.

In Tunisia, up to December, 1942, the GAF liaison officer had not operated directly with the armored combat echelons, but had been depending on information supplied by the commanders of subordinate armored units. Since this information frequently proved unreliable for purposes of effective air support, the air command decided to appoint one of their own officers for direct liaison with the combat echelons. This officer rides in a liaison tank, which operates in the second wave of tanks, near the tank of the armored unit commander.

Assuming, for example, that an attacking tank regiment of an armored division is held up by enemy resistance and immediate air support is needed, the procedure would be as follows. The regimental commander consults with the air liaison officer, and a decision is made as to the air support required. The request for air support is then transmitted by radio to the headquarters of the Fliegerführer (officer in charge of air operations in the area); this message is simultaneously received at the headquarters of the armored division. The message should include the position and type of target to be attacked, the estimated number of aircraft required, the type and height of cloud cover, and the possible opposition to be encountered.

The Fliegerführer then orders, from the airdrome nearest the scene of action, such air support as he thinks necessary, and notifies the liaison officer when the formation is about to take off. Direct communication between the liaison officer and the aircraft is established after the formation is airborne. The liaison officer directs the planes to the target by radio. If, meanwhile, the target has changed position, he indicates its new location. Radio contact is also maintained between the liaison officer, the commander of the tank regiment, and the other tanks.

Comment: The above information seems to bear out reports from other sources concerning German practice in recent operations, and as such, is considered to be worthy of credence.

22. A GERMAN ANTITANK GUN EMPLACEMENT

A report and sketch of a German antitank gun position during World War II, from Tactical and Technical Trends, No. 28, July 1st, 1943.

A sketch of a German diagram of an emplacement for an antitank gun shows some interesting details. The diagram is stated to have been prepared for a defense system based on defense areas. The

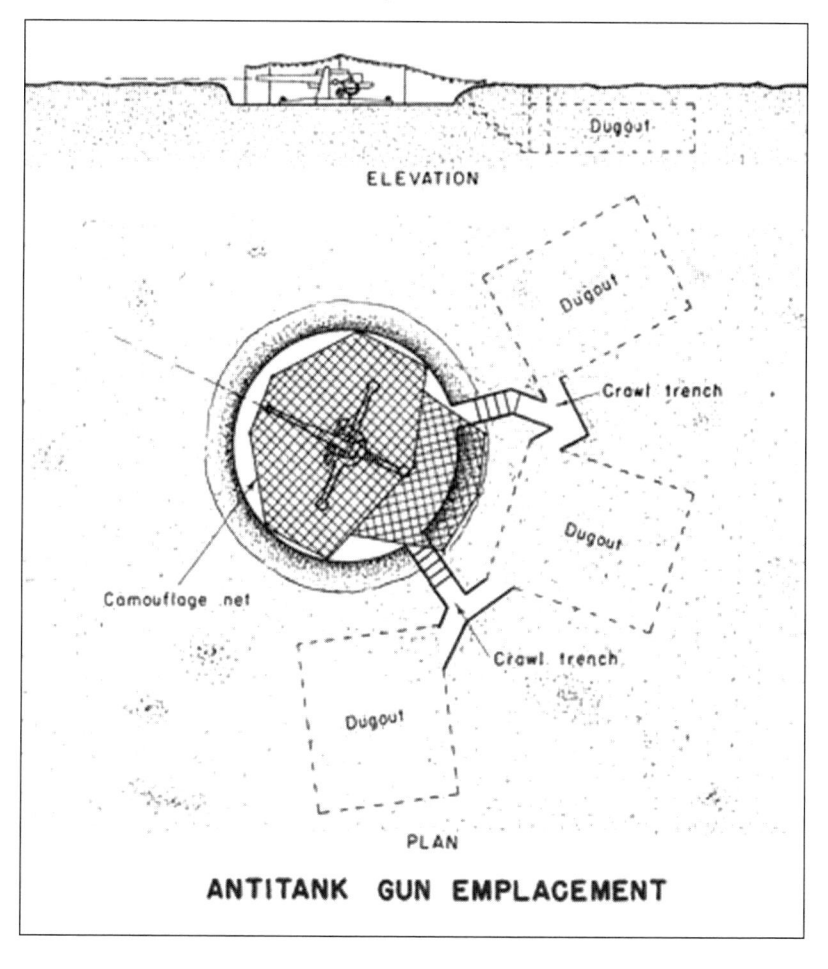

ANTITANK GUN EMPLACEMENT

German document in explanation thereof follows.

"The positions will be arranged in accordance with the following plan:

(a) Field of fire in all directions;
(b) The crew as near as possible to the gun;
(c) Two to three men in one dugout with the dugouts mutually interconnected;
(d) Crawl trenches to the position. This will allow firing in any direction; enable the crew to be ready for action at all times; and permit the men to move about unobserved even during the day."

23. GERMAN 88'S IN TUNISIA

A commander of a U.S. tank regiment in Tunisia reports on German 88-mm AA/AT gun tactics, from Tactical and Technical Trends, No. 28, July 1st, 1943.

A battalion commander of a U.S. tank regiment which saw a lot of action in Tunisia is the source of the following observations on the tactical use of German 88-mm AA/AT guns against tanks and other vehicles.

German antitank gunnery has made our reconnaissance a particularly tough job. They drag their big 88-mm guns (maybe 75's as well—I know they bring 88's) up behind their tanks and drop them in position. Usually the crew digs the gun in a hole 12 by 12 by 6 feet deep, practically covering up the shield and exposing only the barrel of the gun. They are the most wonderful things to camouflage I have ever seen. They are very low to the ground. You can watch the fire coming in; little dust balls on the ground give them away and show how low they are. The gun looks like a pencil or black spot. The shield is level with the piece and all you can effectively see is the tube. Apparently they use mats to hide the muzzle blast. When the Germans go into position they'll hide their guns and tanks in anything, including Arab huts. They dress their personnel in Arab garb while going to and from their positions. We've found these guns particularly hard to locate, and they can break up your entire show if you don't pick them up in time. Once we hunted a gun within a thousand yards for 3 days, and then only found it by spotting the personnel approaching the gun position.

Generally the Germans try to suck you into an antitank gun trap. Their light tanks will bait you in by playing around just outside effective range. When you start after them, they turn tail and draw you in within range of their 88's. First they open up on you with their guns in depth. Then when you try to flank them you find yourself under fire of carefully concealed guns at a shorter range. Don't always bite at the first 88's which shoot at you. There will be several up much closer. The first 88 that barks and the first tank are generally bait. If they stage a night attack or late evening attack, and neither side stays on the battlefield, they will come out and put their 88's in no-man's-land away ahead of their tank positions. In one instance their tanks were within 1,000 yards of a pass, but their guns were 4,000 yards on the other side. Usually the Germans will try to suck you inside of a 1,200-yard range. Over 1,200 yards there is no use in worrying about their antitank fire because it will bounce off the medium tank at that range. Under 1,200 yards, watch out. Their gunnery stinks at long ranges. I feel that our men are better. The Germans frequently use machine guns to range themselves in, and you can duck their shells by watching that machine-gun fire. When they're moving they'll shoot at anything that looks suspicious and they'll generally knock down every Arab house in sight. Sometimes they'll get the range with high-burst smoke shells; three of these in a line is the high sign for the Stukas.

24. ATTACK AGAINST GERMAN HEAVY TANK - PZKW 6

Observer's report on the destruction of two German Tiger tanks by British anti-tank guns in North Africa, from Tactical and Technical Trends, July 29th, 1943.

Construction details about some of the features of the new German heavy tank have already been described in Tactical and Technical Trends (see No. 24, p. 6 and No. 20, p. 7).

The following report by an observer on the Tunisian front furnishes some comments as a guide to training in antitank action against this tank.

It appears that the first of these tanks to be destroyed in this theater were accounted for by British 6-pounders (57-mm). An account of this action, as reported by a British Army Officer, follows:

"The emplaced 6-pounders opened fire at an initial range of 680 yards. The first rounds hit the upper side of the tank at very acute angles and merely nicked the armor. As the tank moved nearer, it turned in such a manner that the third and fourth shots gouged out scallops of armor, the fifth shot went almost through and the next three rounds penetrated completely and stopped the tank. The first complete penetration was at a range of 800 yards, at an angle of impact of 30 degrees from normal, through homogeneous armor 82-mm (approximately 3 1/3 inches) thick. Ammunition used was the 57-mm semi-AP solid shot.

"One element of this action contains an important lesson that should be brought to the attention of all AT elements and particularly tank destroyer units.

(a) "The British gunners did not open until the enemy tank was well within effective range.

(b) "In addition to opening fire with the primary weapon — the 57-mm — the AT unit also opened with intense light machine-gun fire which forced the tank to button up and in effect blinded him. His vision apparently became confused and he was actually traversing his gun away from the AT guns when he was knocked out for good.

(c) "Once they opened fire, the British gunners really poured it on and knocked out one more heavy tank and six PzKw 3s. Also, for good measure, one armored car."

The conclusions to be drawn from this action, according to the British officer quoted, are:

(a) "The unobstructed vision of the gunner in a tank destroyer gives him a very real advantage over his opponent squinting through the periscope or narrow vision slits of a tank.

(b) "The tank destroyer unit must force the enemy tank to 'button up' by intense fire from every weapon he has, including machine-guns, tommy guns, and rifles."

The size and weight of a tank such as the PzKw 6 present many problems. It has been indicated from unofficial enemy sources that extensive reconnaissance of terrain, bridges, etc., was necessary before operations with this tank could be undertaken. Bridges have to be reinforced in many cases, and soil conditions must be good for its effective operation. It can therefore be assumed that its field of operation is limited.

Reports so far indicate that the use of this tank is chiefly to support other armored units, including employment as mobile artillery. As a support tank it is always in rear of lighter units. In one reported skirmish in Tunisia, the lighter units formed the spear-head; as soon as enemy tanks were decoyed into range the lighter tanks fanned out, leaving the heavier tanks in the rear to engage the enemy units.

The PzKw 6 is now considered a standard German tank. Present production figures are believed to be at a maximum of 800 per month.

25. NOTES ON SECURITY FROM THE MIDDLE EAST

A report with British notes on field security in the Middle East, from the Intelligence Bulletin, March 1943.

1. INTRODUCTION

"Security in the military sense consists not only of denying information to the enemy, but also preserving information about the enemy which is of use to ourselves." This statement sums up the British attitude regarding security. All members of the armed forces are continually reminded of the importance of acquiring and guarding enemy documents and materiel so that they may be studied by the proper experts, even though the items may not seem important in themselves. In the following notes the British illustrate very clearly how troops in the field are in a position to cooperate with intelligence officers in preserving information about the enemy, and why the individual soldier is to regard such cooperation as "must."

2. PRESERVING ENEMY AIRCRAFT

Proper guarding of enemy aircraft which has come into our hands is essential. It is especially important to insure against the looting of such planes. Personnel have sometimes been heard to ask "Why bother? Don't we know all about enemy aircraft already?" No, we certainly don't! And even if we did, it could only be because flawless security work had been done in the past.

As an example of the information that can be obtained from a crash, consider the case of a Heinkel which was shot down by night fighter action. This aircraft crashed in flames, and the wreckage was spread over a square mile. At first glance, it seemed as though nothing remained but charred and unrecognizable fragments. Nevertheless, examination by the proper authorities quickly revealed new points of technical value, as well as production details about where and when the engines and various other parts were made. In addition, valuable papers were retrieved. It cannot be overemphasized that even a scrap of paper may be of value from an intelligence point of view.

At the moment, we are searching for an important development in German radio. A certain apparatus is fitted with a destroying device, and if anyone should happen to tamper with one of these devices on an enemy aircraft which has come into our possession, the apparatus will be lost and essential information along with it.

Therefore, individuals who tamper with items of enemy equipment are doing the Axis a service and are slowing down our own war effort.

3. SAFEGUARDING ENEMY DOCUMENTS

During the Libyan campaign a New Zealand intelligence officer made quick use of some maps that a German major general had not been given time to destroy, and therefore was able to inform the New Zealand commander that the German 21st Armored Division was due to arrive in the immediate future. The New Zealand general was able to plan his strategy accurately.

A truck serving as an office for the adjutant general and quartermaster of the German 15th Armored Division was captured intact during the Libyan campaign. Intelligence officers rushed its contents back to G.H.Q. by air. There probably had been no greater find in the course of the war up to that time. Not only did the truck contain documents of enemy operational value, but also up-to-date German manuals, publications, and other items, which were enormously useful. Thus, from the military intelligence point of view, it is not an exaggeration to say that the contents of a single truck preserved intact may influence the whole course of the war.

The widely dispersed vehicles of a Panzer Division scattered over a wide area in order to minimise the ever present possibility of air attack.

On October 17, 1942, an alert trooper of the 7th Hussars snatched a document from a German prisoner who was in the act of tearing it up. This bit of quick thinking enabled us to identify and locate several German units at a time when information was more than usually scarce.

When charred remnants of paper are salvaged, the complete destruction of which has been prevented just in time, it often turns out that they contain some useful items of information.

Whenever documents are captured, every possible step must be taken to destroy all evidence pointing to the fact that they have been captured; that is, the office in which they were found must be burned, the officer from whose person they were taken must be removed from the scene, and so on.

4. THE SOUVENIR HABIT

A desire to keep captured documents and equipment as souvenirs sometimes results in the loss of much information which would be helpful to the armed forces as a whole. This point is well illustrated by the case of a battalion commander who, in forwarding his unit war diaries to second echelon, made a special request that certain attached captured documents should not be removed from the file in which he was sending them. It was discovered that these documents had been captured sometime before, and unfortunately had never been passed on to the proper authority. Soldiers sending parcels home have included the following articles as souvenirs:

(1) Binoculars and compasses, of which our own fighting troops are short.
(2) Many rounds of ammunition (for a German antitank gun) that our own tank designers needed urgently for test purposes.
(3) An electrical gyroscopic compass, also urgently wanted for research.
(4) Enemy tank logbooks giving us valuable information regarding enemy tank production.
(5) Many useful photographs of enemy equipment about which our information was not yet complete.
(6) Valuable items of signal equipment.
(7) Specimens of Axis food which would have provided useful clues for our blockade authorities.
(8) Many types of fuzes, or igniters, and detonators, some of which were new to us and all of which were helpful in some way.
(9) Italian shoulder straps and a German football jersey with a badge, which gave us valuable identifications, including the fact that a new unit had been formed.

Erwin Rommel explains his strategy to a staff officer, June 1942.

26. GERMAN MINE FIELDS IN LIBYA

The following report on German mine tactics in Libya during World War II was originally published in Tactical and Technical Trends, No. 1, June 18th, 1942.

German mine fields encountered in the Tobruk area are reported to have been, with very few exceptions, combinations of anti-tank and anti-personnel mines. A row of "Sperrmine" anti-personnel mines, called "S" mines, with push igniters was frequently laid in front of the Teller mines (platter shaped anti-tank mine, weighing about 10 lbs.). This apparently was intended to make the work of taking up the minefield more dangerous.

Trip wires intended to give warning of the approach of hostile troops were also utilized. It is reported that "T" mines are usually laid with the top of the igniter flush with the ground and the earth smoothed back into place. No elaborate concealment has been encountered and the disturbed earth usually makes the mines easy to locate. No pull-igniters have been found in the cavities provided for them in the side and base of "T" mines although the Germans are known to have used this type of igniter in the area.

In one case a field of "T" mines was found to have been arranged for deliberate firing, and engineer reconnaissance discovered electric leads connected to the arming points in the sides of the mines. They were wired in parallel to enable the mines to be fired singly or in groups.

"S" mines are usually laid with only an inch of the antennae visible, and the disturbed earth carefully smoothed back into place. Nevertheless, the disturbed earth usually makes their location easy, as no elaborate attempt at concealment has been encountered.

Push, pull, and pedal-types of this mine have been encountered, the two former predominating.

27. SMALL-ARMS FIRE AGAINST LOW-FLYING AIRCRAFT

The following intelligence report on German and British small-arms fire against ground-attack aircraft in World War II was originally published in Tactical and Technical Trends, No. 9, October 8th, 1942.

Small-arms fire against low-flying aircraft has been used extensively in North Africa.

It is reported that the Germans make the best use of this fire, though the British use it effectively. Effectiveness depends upon the training of the soldiers, their watchfulness for approaching aircraft, and the refusal to be stampeded and run when attacked.

The fighter pilots who carry out low-flying attacks consider this type of mission the most dangerous of all. The effectiveness of small-arms fire by Axis ground troops is illustrated by the history of the use of the Boston support bomber. This bomber, though built and designed for low-flying attacks, is being used at from 10,000 to 12,000 feet. It proved to be very vulnerable to small-arms fire from 50 feet to 100 feet. As the altitude of the attack was raised, the aircraft came within heavy machine-gun range and, later, light and medium antiaircraft fire, until 10,000 feet was considered the safest altitude.

As to the effectiveness of the British fire, one observer reports having seen three out of six Fiat CR-42 Italian fighters shot down within 5 minutes by small-arms fire while carrying out a low ground-strafing attack near Knightsbridge. It must be remembered, however, that the CR-42 is an obsolescent aircraft and that all of them were flying at about 100 feet, which is too high for such an attack.

28. SECURITY MEASURES OF A GERMAN ARMORED DIVISION

The following intelligence report on German security measures originally appeared in Tactical and Technical Trends, No. 12, November 19th, 1942. The report is based on captured orders from the commander of the German 15th Panzer Division in North Africa.

In the late spring of 1942, both the Germans and the British on the Gazala—Bir Hacheim line were building up strength for offensive action and, at the same time, organizing their own defensive systems to repulse the expected enemy attack. A captured German order issued by the Commander of the 15th Armored Division contains several interesting notes on these German defensive preparations.

Comparing the position of the division to that of a "spider lying in wait... for its victim," the commander ordered all elements of the division to be ready for action as follows:

(a) All front-line troops, immediately upon attack by the enemy;
(b) A specially designated task force, within an hour;
(c) The remainder of the division, within 3 hours.

Instructions were given for thorough ground reconnaissance to be carried out by all units down to and including platoons. Artillery observers were ordered to take positions much farther forward than normally, since "otherwise, after the first shot, dust develops and there is no possibility for direction of fire."

Apparently a tank company, in addition to the normal armored-car patrols, was to be held in readiness for action at all times. This company, however, was not to be committed unless the enemy attacked in force, and above all, was not to engage routine enemy patrols.

Just as the tank company was to be held as a reserve, the

remainder of the division's tanks was not to be committed until the artillery and Panzerjäger units had engaged the enemy. Apparently, the German commander expected the British attack to consist primarily of tanks.

In addition to the regular minefields, dummy minefields were ordered laid. The commander emphasized that a great deal more attention should be given to making these fields realistic, pointing out that a captured British document indicated that the German dummy minefields were ordinarily too easily distinguished from the real ones.

Knowing that the British had a justifiable fear of the 88-mm gun, the commander ordered that dummy 88's be constructed with trucks and old telephone poles.

In addition to these measures of deception, dust generators (no description given) were to be used for simulating vehicle movements; and captured British trucks were to be camouflaged as tanks.

Great emphasis was laid on utilizing existing materiel to the utmost to achieve greater combat effectiveness. Unit leaders were requested to submit suggestions on how a larger amount of ammunition and fuel could be carried by the existing transport facilities. In this connection they were asked to discard all possible material and equipment which would be unnecessary for combat.

29. GERMAN CONSTRUCTION AND DEVELOPMENT OF STRONGPOINT

The following U.S. military report on German methods in the construction and development of strongpoints was originally published in Tactical and Technical Trends, No. 14, December 17th, 1942.

The following steps are reported to be typical of German methods in the construction and development of a strongpoint.

STEP I

All three positions must be chosen so that each has an all-round field of fire.

Whenever possible, rocky ground which is likely to be exposed to heavy enemy fire must be avoided. Officers themselves should lay out the positions with the greatest care.

STEP II

Communication trenches, 5 feet in depth, between the three positions and dugout will be added.

Later, the trenches will be covered with boards and stones in order to make them splinter-proof and difficult to recognize from the air.

STEP III

(a) Wiring of the strong point;
(b) Laying of antitank mines in the wire;
(c) Wiring of individual positions (antitank and machine gun);
(d) Covering of communication trenches between the positions.

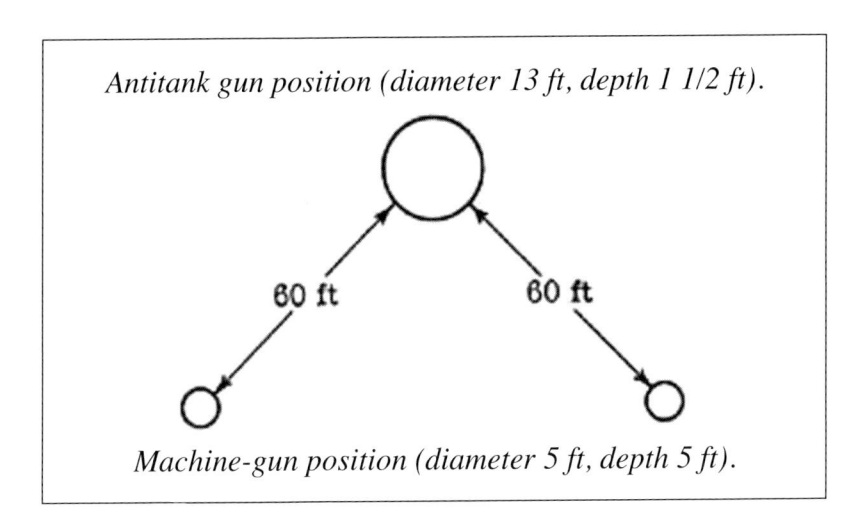

Antitank gun position (diameter 13 ft, depth 1 1/2 ft).

Machine-gun position (diameter 5 ft, depth 5 ft).

60 ft   60 ft

Step I

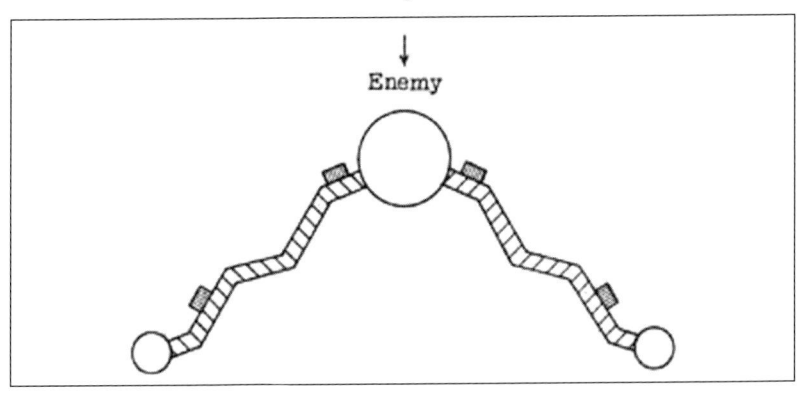

Enemy

Step II

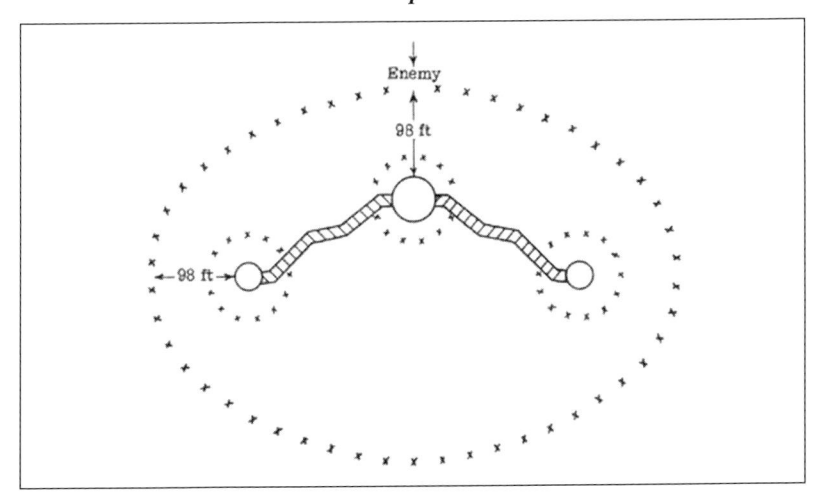

Enemy
98 ft
←98 ft→

Step III

30. SUMMARY AND EVALUATION OF OPERATIONS IN EGYPT

The following report on the Battle of El Alamein was originally published in Tactical and Technical Trends, No. 15, December 31st, 1942.

OCTOBER 23 TO NOVEMBER 7, 1942

a. Summary of Operations

On October 23, Axis armored divisions were disposed in two groups as follows: the 21st Panzer and the Italian Ariete in rear of the south end of the line; the 15th Panzer, the Italian Littorio, and the German 90th Light (less certain reconnaissance elements), in rear of the north end of the line.

Beginning October 27, the Axis armored forces which had been concentrated in the north counterattacked vigorously, particularly against the north end of the British line. This was unsuccessful due to prior Axis losses and stiff British resistance.

On October 30, the 21st Panzer Division moved north and joined the 90th Light Division and the two armored divisions in that area; the Trieste Division (motorized), the only available reserve on the entire front, was committed in the north.

By the morning of November 1, the British completed regrouping the X Armored Corps, and in the evening the Corps attacked due west. The main effort of this attack was directed frontally against the 15th Panzer Division and the Italian Littorio (Armored) Division. Both of these Axis divisions suffered heavy casualties. The British attack penetrated, into the Axis rear areas and isolated one regiment of the German 164th Division along the coast. The 21st Panzer Division at this time was also along the coast, west of the 164th Division. The Axis forces counterattacked desperately and lost heavily in tanks and antitank guns in combat between armored units. Although suffering heavy losses, the 90th Light and the two German Panzer divisions with their depleted forces succeeded in withdrawing to the west.

A large proportion of the Italian forces in the south, lacking transportation, ceased resistance and they, together with miscellaneous German troops, were captured by the British XIII Corps.

b. Change in German Commanders

It is interesting to note that a change in German commanders during this period probably had a marked influence on the Axis conduct of the operation. At the beginning of the period, General Stumme was in command of the Afrika Korps in Marshal Rommel's absence. It was during his command that the Axis armor was split into two groups. On October 26, Stumme was killed in action and General Thoma took command. He initiated the concentration of his armored units for employment as a striking force.

c. Evaluation of Axis Tactics

Concentration of effort has always been a basic German tactical principle. It is almost axiomatic with German commanders to employ their armored units, specifically tanks, in mass to deliver hammer blows.

Hence it is difficult to understand why General Stumme divided his armored force into two parts, one south and the other north, without keeping an armored force in general reserve to deal with a British breakthrough. Perhaps terrain and lack of adequate facilities dictated his choice. Nevertheless, his reported disposition against an alert and well-equipped enemy possessing superior air power invited the Axis defeat that followed.

General Thoma's concentration of his armored forces apparently came too late. The British not only were prepared to take on the Axis counterattacks but they were able to renew the

Rommel and Generalmajor von Bismarck during a staff conference in the Libyan desert during mid 1942.

offensive at the proper moment, when the Axis forces were disorganized and expended as a result of these counterattacks.

d. Evaluation of British Tactics

Improvements in British tactics have been noted in the following respects:

(1) Intense and effective use of artillery against tanks and antitank guns.

(2) Judicious use of armored units concentrated for mass employment.

(3) Coordination between tanks and infantry movements.

The conduct of this campaign by the British was at marked variance with that of other desert operations. Previously, armored regiments, reinforced, were used independently as striking forces, but in this action the British X Corps, composed of two armored divisions and one motorized division, was used as a unit. This change in tactics was without doubt due in part to the recent sweeping changes in British High Command in the Middle East; but lessons learned in previous desert operations probably played a more important part.

31. GERMAN 21ST ARMORED DIVISION—DIVISION SUPPLY

The following brief report on the supply elements of the German 21st Panzer Division was originally published in Tactical and Technical Trends, *No. 16, January 14th, 1943.*

The German Afrika Korps has, at least until somewhat recently, operated very successfully in North Africa. No small part of this success can be attributed to an efficient German supply system.

According to prisoner of war statements the division supply elements of the German 21st Armored Division (Afrika Korps) consisted of a supply company and 12 supply columns.

The 12 supply columns consisted of 4 heavy columns, 7 light columns, and 1 gasoline and oil column. A heavy column had 24 vehicles with an aggregate capacity of 60 tons; a light column had 12 vehicles with an aggregate capacity of 30 tons. The 12 columns, exclusive of the gasoline and oil column, thus has a total cargo capacity of 450 tons.

The supply company was actually an Arbeitskompanie or labor company. Its function was to cooperate with the division supply columns by carrying out such tasks as unloading, establishing dumps, maintenance, etc. The strength of the company was estimated at from 200 to 250 men.

The division was reported to maintain 3 supply dumps—one each for Class I, Class III, and Class V supplies—which were close together and forward of which supplies were never moved by division transport. It was the function of unit transport to move supplies to the front from these dumps. The operating radius of both the supply columns and supply company was said to be from 100 to 200 kilometers (60 to 120 miles).

32. WATER SUPPLY OF A GERMAN TANK BATTALION IN LIBYA

The following U.S. military report on the water supplies required for a German panzer battalion in Libya was originally published in Tactical and Technical Trends, No. 16, January 14th, 1943.

The following report gives one example of the problem of supply of troops operating in the desert. A German tank battalion, leaving Tripoli for El Agheila in 1941, took the following water supplies for three days' march:

Unit	For Engine Cooling	For Washing Purposes
Headquarters Company	122*	150
5th Company (light)	111	100
6th Company (light)	114	100
8th Company (medium)	93	100
Total	**440**	**450**

All figures refer to the number of containers carried by the particular unit; each container held about 5 gallons.

The above containers were distributed throughout the battalion as follows: one container per car; two containers per truck, half-track, armored car and light tank; three containers per medium tank.

This quantity of water represented only one-third of the total amount that had to be taken. The remainder was carried in a special water column, and provided about 2 gallons of water per man for the three-day period. The distribution among vehicles was in proportion to the number of personnel carried.

Each company carried 130 containers with water for cooking. These containers were carried on the supply trucks which

A Panzer III undergoing refueling and re-arming in a rudimentary camp, April 1942.

accompanied the field kitchens.

The total amount of water carried by the battalion was as follows:

Cooling	5,100 gallons
Washing	2,250 gallons
Cooking and Drinking	4,465 gallons
Total	**11,815 gallons**

A comparison of the amounts per man per day between the British and Germans is as follows: the Germans allow 2/3 of a gallon for washing, 1 1/3 for cooking and drinking; the British allow 1 gallon for washing, and 1 for cooking and drinking.

More from the same series

Most books from the 'Hitler's War Machine' series are edited and endorsed by Emmy Award winning film maker and military historian Bob Carruthers, producer of Discovery Channel's Line of Fire and Weapons of War and BBC's Both Sides of the Line. Long experience and strong editorial control gives the military history enthusiast the ability to buy with confidence.

Tiger I in Combat	Tiger I Crew Manual	Panzers at War 1939-1942	Panzers at War 1943-1945
Wolf Pack - the U boats	Poland 1939	Luftwaffe Combat Reports	Eastern Front Night
Eastern Front Encirclement	Panzer Combat Reports	The Panther V in Combat	German Tank Hunters
The Afrika Korps in Combat	Panzers I & II	Panzer III	Panzer IV

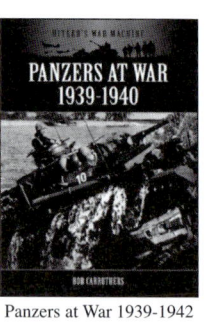

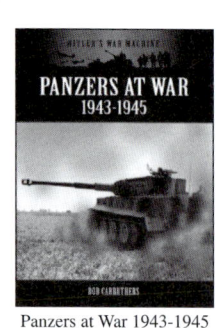

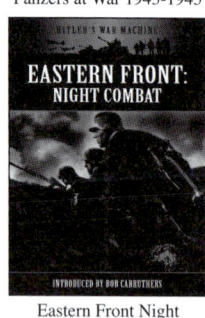

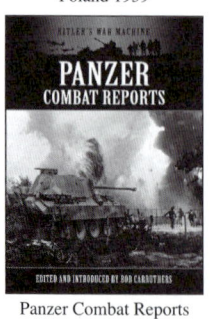

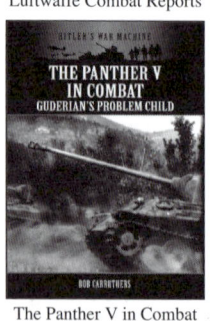

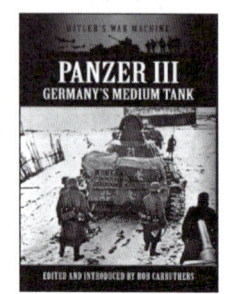

For more information visit www.pen-and-sword.co.uk